Reach
Your
Career
Dreams

Reach Your Career Dreams

CareerTrack's Handbook for Professional Women

Edited by
Diane Hudson and Jan Simon

CAREERTRACK PUBLICATIONS • BOULDER, COLORADO

Book and Cover Design: Bobbi Benson
Composition/Graphic Artist: Cheryl Warner
Typography: Anne Vaughan
Illustration: Barry Zaid

Type: English Times Roman
Library of Congress Catalog Card Number: 86-72918
Printed First Edition in the United States of America
ISBN: 0-943066-19-0

Table of Contents

Introduction ix

1 Set High, Yet Achievable Goals 1

2 Network To Get Known............................. 12

3 Project A High Profile............................. 30

4 Communicate With Power......................... 47

5 Dealing With Conflict Confidently 59

6 Master Organization Politics....................... 75

7 Negotiate With Skill................................ 99

8 Make Persuasive Presentations 111

9 Take Risks Decisively 136

10 Get (Or Advance) Your College Degree
   Without Classes.................................. 155

11 Manage Your Stress And Energy Level 173

12 Nurture The Roots Of Success..................... 195

Introduction

Lee Strasberg, the founder of the legendary Actors' Studio in New York, once said, "If we cannot see the possibility of greatness, how can we dream of it?"

This book is about making your dreams come true.

It's filled with specific techniques leading to one thing: your success.

What is success? As you'll read in the following chapters, it all comes down to a simple, yet powerful concept: being all you can and want to be.

Don't expect magic potions. There simply aren't any. What you'll get from this book is more powerful than magic. Twelve specific steps to your success. Follow them and nothing on this planet will keep you from achieving your dreams.

We asked CareerTrack's hottest women seminar trainers to author *Reach Your Career Dreams.* These women are, quite frankly, eleven of the best career development specialists in the country. They've personally trained hundreds of thousands of women in the skills of success. (CareerTrack is producer of *Power Communication Skills* and *Image & Self-Projection,* the most popular women's seminars of all time.)

The result is a step-by-step guide that explains the basics. And the basics are exactly what you need to fulfill your career dreams: Step #1, Set high, yet achievable goals. Step #2, Network to get known. Step #3, Project a high profile. Step #4, Communicate with power. Step #5, Deal with conflict confidently. Step #6, Master organization politics. Step #7, Negotiate with skill. Step #8, Make persuasive presentations. Step #9, Take risks decisively. Step #10, Get (or advance) your college degree without classes. Step #11, Manage your stress and energy levels. Step #12, Nurture your roots of success.

Realistic. Concentrated. And right on target.

We're proud of the CareerTrack experts who created this book. As we said earlier, they're among the best in the business.

But you know what's so terrific about them? Each of them

writes from her heart. They haven't cut and pasted information from college textbooks or business manuals.

They've lived it.

And from living it, they've learned. They've made mistakes. They've cried. They've failed.

And they've triumphed.

So will you. Here's to your career dreams.

Diane Hudson
Jan Simon
Boulder, Colorado
November — 1986

Reach Your Career Dreams

Step #1
Set High, Yet Achievable Goals

by Pamela Pearce

Where are you in your life right now? Are you living it on your own terms? Or have you sacrificed too much, too long for too little?

These are important questions for the woman who is sincerely interested in success.

In this chapter you will learn a four-step plan you can follow to create the life you want — and feel good about it. In our society too many women are either unhappy with their situations or are not getting the support they need to do what they want to do. Alice, for example, has started her own business and needs all the support she can get. Yet every night when she comes home tired, her husband asks, "Hey, honey, when are you going to get a real job?"

Follow the life planning system outlined here and you will join a prestigious group of people: self-disciplined, confident, creative and determined. They can point to their lives and proclaim, "I am a success."

1

Step 1: Establish A Purpose

Do you ever feel that life has not yet started for you? Do you ever feel that no matter how much you achieve, something still is missing? If so, ask yourself: "What is my purpose in life?" This is the toughest and most important question you will ever ask. Activities without a sense of overall purpose are meaningless, like the accountant endlessly crunching numbers with no sense of the company big picture. Purpose fits all the pieces together. It functions as the cornerstone of your existence.

Most businesswomen are familiar with the concept of purpose. No business interested in long-term success, for example, would operate without a "corporate mission." From that mission each department in the company draws its goals'and objectives. And to the degree each department is guided in its progress, the business will succeed.

You are the president of a corporation called "Your Life." It is your responsibility to establish a purpose or mission. It is also your responsibility to freely choose resources such as a mate, children, a job, friends, etc., to help you get what you want. If the resources you choose are consistent with your overall purpose in life, and you respect and nurture them, you will be successful.

The following diagram will help you visualize how the pieces fit together.

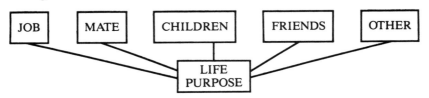

Purpose gives your life balance and perspective. It also helps you set meaningful short- and long-term goals. And it helps you channel your energy constructively. Copy the following equation on a card, carry it with you and read it daily.

Purpose = Balance = Success.

A well-thought-out, self-serving purpose can help you make decisions that you otherwise might put off or handle poorly. Carol, for example, is a young professional woman with a husband and small child. Her purpose in life is "to maintain a balance by maintaining mental health." When Carol's mother asked her to invite her 17-year-old sister, who had problems with discipline and drugs and who had already caused upheaval in two homes, to live with her, Carol was able to say no. Why? Because she studied the situation through her stated purpose: maintaining her own mental health. Carol knew that she loved her sister and wanted to help, but she also knew that bringing undue stress into her young family was not the answer.

You can find countless examples of women who have not established a self-serving purpose in life and get stuck in a downward spiral of confusion and dissatisfaction. Think of the worn-out mother who spent twenty-five years sacrificing for a husband and children who showed no appreciation and finally left her all alone. Twenty-five years is a long time to go without satisfaction.

Commitment

A major part of creating a purpose for your life is commitment. Purpose gives your life direction; commitment makes it work. Commitment is realizing that you are free to choose what you want to do, but once the choice is made, it is up to you to keep your word to yourself. For example, if Carol, whose purpose in life is to keep mentally healthy, decided to have an affair with the leader of a motorcycle gang, she would not be living up to her personal commitment to stay away from craziness.

The system is foolproof only when you follow the rules. But it is also flexible in that it allows for mature compromise. This is how it works. Marsha is a medical doctor who is heavily involved in cancer research. Her well-thought-out purpose in life states, "My purpose is to surround myself with people who have my best interest in mind." She has maintained the integrity of that decision through three job changes and one poor marriage. She is currently married to a wonderful man. But Marsha has a problem. She has recently taken a senior research position which she adores. The job is challenging, full of variety and freedom, and it is just political enough to be interesting. The problem? Her department head. He is a shrewd, self-serving egotist who is intimidated by smart, assertive, successful women. He does everything in his power to undermine her success. Marsha experiences him not as a genuine obstacle to her research but as a major psychological thorn in her side. The man goes through her notes when she is out, gives her curt answers, withholds information and makes disparaging remarks about her competence behind her back. She has addressed the situation in a variety of ways to no avail. Marsha desperately wants to keep her "almost perfect" position, but doing so would mean compromising her need to have a supportive environment. What should she do?

Compromising one's life purpose is no major cause for alarm. You write your script and you can change it when necessary. The trouble starts when a person is not mature enough to handle the change. For example, if Marsha would choose to stay in her position despite the frustrations, there is a good chance she would begin to bring those frustrations home and contaminate her marriage. On the other hand, if she chose to behave maturely, she would recognize that she made her bed, so to speak, and must lie in it. Healthy venting is okay in this life planning system, but destructive complaining and resentment are out of the question.

The Course of Your Life

Remember in school when you learned not to color outside of the lines, even though you knew it would be fun? Remember when you were told to stop daydreaming in class, even though you found it stimulating? Grandmother convinced you that "girls don't grow up to be astronauts" even though you thought you could, so you became less. Your parents told you that security was more important than seeking adventure, so you married the guy next door and now try to ignore the empty feeling inside.

Some women even act as though they doubt they have a right to do what they want to do. I'm reminded of a story told of a brilliant young economist who had it all: a good job in her father's bank, a handsome husband, fun-loving friends, money and a promising future. But she chose to end her life because, as the note said, "My life has been for others. I have been living other people's goals, and life for me has become meaningless." Money, opportunity and attention don't always mean that you are a success. Doing the best you can at what you want, in a way that brings you the support you need from others, is success. For insight into the course your life has taken, seriously consider the following questions:

a. What did your family want you to be (include personal characteristics they valued)?

b. What groups, behaviors, attitudes, professions did/do your friends value?

c. What do you *not* want to do with your life and what characteristics in a person do you *not* value?

d. What do you think you would really like to do with your life? "My purpose in life is..."

How do you feel about your answers? If you have clarified that you are on the right track, great. If you realized you need to change direction, great. It's never too late to change things. Take yourself to a quiet place and just sit. Consider the above questions carefully. Think about your purpose in life while you are brushing your teeth or riding in the car or especially when you feel discouraged, frustrated and angry. Consider and reflect and even talk to others if necessary until you capture the essence of life for you and crystallize a direction. Once you do, things will begin to fall into place.

Step 2: Choose the Right Resources and Nurture Them

The clearer you are about what you want in life and the resources you need, the higher your probability of success. Circumstances will mysteriously seem to present themselves for your benefit. Money will become available. The personal contact you needed to make will call you. You inquire about a dream job and it happens they were looking for a person just like you. With patience and experience you will learn to trust the universe to help you. But once you have set your course and identified support systems you must be willing to invest in them.

For example, if you decided to plant a garden in your backyard you would first identify resources or tools to help you. You might need a shovel for the big chunks of dirt, a pair of gloves and a wheelbarrow. You don't have gloves so you go to the hardware store and get a pair, but ignore the other two items because you know they are in the shed where you put them last year.

Come Saturday morning you don your gardening gloves and bounce out to get your other tools. You fling open the shed door and gasp with alarm. The shovel has been sitting under a leak in the roof for months and is now rusted beyond repair and the wheelbarrow is gone! (You later learn it had been stolen.) Your day is ruined.

The same thing can happen in life itself: The best laid plans can be shattered if you fail to care for your resources. How many relationships and jobs turned sour because the people involved took them for granted and focused attention on other things? Truly successful people maintain an active involvement in all the key roles they play. They treat their resources with respect.

People are your biggest resource. The relationships you build and cultivate will sustain you in times of need, connect you with opportunity and bring you love, laughter and success. But when you neglect your coworkers or your family or even your relationship with yourself, you undermine your own success. You can't expect to have your tools ready and waiting to help you when you have left them unattended in the shed.

The best way to nurture a resource is to establish a relationship in which there is growth. In order for that to happen, you need goals.

Step 3: Set Goals

It takes skill to set a goal. Many people act as though they have plucked their goals out of the air. They arbitrarily decide they want a certain car, mate, batch of friends, lifestyle, job, etc., and they look around for ways to get them. That approach to goal setting is putting the cart before the horse. First, establish a purpose in life. Second, identify the key resources to help you live out that purpose. Third, set goals for each resource that are consistent with your overall purpose.

What specific goals have you set for yourself in your career, with your family, your friends, your religion and in the area of personal development? Have you written them down? The only goals most people have written appear in their school yearbooks in a very nebulous form. "I want to be happy and make a lot of money." Your goals need to be specific, measurable, realistic and desirable to you. For example, "I want to be happy, which to me means..." and "to make a lot of money, which to me means..." Once you have established a goal you must design a plan to meet it.

Right now take a moment and create one long- and one short-term goal in each of your key life roles. Consider such roles as your job, mate, children, friends, etc. Make sure the short is related to the long and that each goal is consistent with your life purpose.

Here's a helpful hint: break your long-term goals into short-term deadlines — weekly. You'll be pleasantly surprised by the results you'll get. Give yourself lots of deadlines; in fact, write them down in weekly goal-setting sessions (remember, you've made a commitment to success).

As an example, let's say you've set as one of your long-term goals to assume leadership of a volunteer organization in three years. What do you need to do *right now* to achieve that goal? Serving on various committees, getting to know key people in the organization, and reading about leaders are just a few of the weekly goals you can set for yourself in order to reach your long-term goal. You'll be giving yourself small, immediate victories that keep you enthusiastic and focused on moving ahead.

Congratulations! You are on your way to creating a solid life plan. Now take a moment and review those goals again. Are they risky or have you played it safe in your planning process? Did you decide to marry a doctor or to be one? Don't be surprised if you realize your goals are modest. Given the conditioning you were subjected to as a female in a male-dominated society, you are doing well to have established any specific goals. Most women spend more time planning a two-week vacation than they do planning their lives. When it comes to life goals they tend to rely on hope and fantasy.

Goal setting takes courage. Someone or something will always be around to trigger that little negative voice in your head that says, "You can't do that." Let your own voice of confidence and determination speak louder. Let the brave child in you, who would try anything, remind you of the truth about obstacles: "They are meant to challenge, not destroy you." Reaching your goals means anticipating obstacles and being ready to deal with them.

Learn all you can about men and women who have achieved great things in the face of tremendous adversity. Read everything you can get your hands on that will help you dream and visualize your own success. Take advantage of cassette tape learning. You can listen to a cassette while driving in the car, getting ready in the morning or even writing a letter to a friend. You don't need to be concentrating totally for the message to sink in, but you do need at least six or seven repetitions of a concept to internalize it solidly.

Also, don't be so reasonable!! When setting goals in the key areas of your life, try being unreasonable. "But we have never even considered taking a trip down the Amazon before." "But what would the boss say if I told her I wanted to take on such a project?" Do you want to break some rules? Break them. Do you want to take some real risks? Take them.

"Good" Excuses

How do you really feel about your job right now? How about your relationships? Do you like the way you are treated by your lover, husband, children, friends, etc.? Do you want to make some changes? What is stopping you? I know. You have a whole closet full of good excuses. Certainly you wouldn't let a bad excuse stop you from something as important as success.

We all know women who have good excuses for not doing something. They lie to themselves and others. They say one thing and do another. They describe to us in detail the plot of their new book and never pick up a pen. They promise themselves to switch jobs, get a divorce, stop smoking, come visit you, go on a diet, start their own business, spend a month out of the country, but they never do. These women seem to get more satisfaction out of breaking their commitments than following through. In fact, the only progress they seem to make is finding new people to whom they can tell their story.

When you see a woman in this position you can usually say, "There goes a loser." There goes a woman who has decided to live by the principle of "no result + a good excuse = a result." Just remember: when you choose an excuse for not succeeding, you choose the end result.

If you sincerely wish to improve your life you must follow through with the commitments you make — even after the feelings you had when you made them are gone. You must state clearly and concisely, "This is my goal and this is what I am going to do to get it."

If, for example, your goal is to hold a job where you can be direct and up front with your boss, then when interviewing for a new position, you must get agreement to this kind of relationship before considering any job. You must state your requirement and the consequences of a broken agreement. If the agreement is broken it is your responsibility to follow through on your end of the bargain. The same is true with any contract you make in life. As ancient wisdom goes, "If you say you know but do not do, then you do not yet know." People who fail once and learn from the mistake are winners, but failures make the same mistakes over and over. They resist doing what they need to do to win on their own terms. Styles vary but failures have one thing in common: poor self-esteem. And just like a broken dam will unleash a flood of destruction, shattered self-esteem will weaken and erode the psychological barriers that keep the will to fail in its proper place. To win in life you must have healthy self-esteem or you will ultimately end up a victim.

If you suspect your self-esteem is not as strong as it could be, find a resource that will help you strengthen it. Seek counseling, go to seminars, read biographies, keep a journal, meditate, pray, build nurturing friendships, associate with winners and stay alert to the symptoms of failure, which include substance abuse (drugs, cigarettes and alcohol) and rationalization.

Even Charles Shultz, the cartoonist, has made fun of the way we can fool ourselves into believing we are working toward success when all we are doing is being foolish. Peppermint Patty is in class talking to her teacher:

"My report, ma'am? No, it isn't ready.

"Well, you see, my binder is a three-ring binder. And this filler paper I bought by mistake has only two holes.

"Anyway, I sat up all last night punching new holes in all these pages so they'd fit into the binder.

"The hard part was cutting out and pasting little pieces of paper over the old holes."

Failures busy themselves with thousands of mundane details and never do anything of consequence. Their substitutions masquerade as success and they become obsessed with protecting them. They rationalize their poor choices by saying, "I'm so busy taking care of the boss, doing paperwork, getting organized — how could anybody expect me to do more?" What they are really saying is, "I have chosen the wrong path but I am too afraid to change."

If failures could only learn to imitate the simplest laws of nature. Water, for example, takes the path of least resistance on its journey to the sea. When it comes to a rock, it simply flows around it. Failures don't do that. If they have a specific destination at all and run into an obstacle — a rock — they do not flow. They create a relationship with the rock. They then seek out other failures and complain about their rocks together. They tell each other they are winners for hanging in there. How ridiculous and sad! No wonder the poet wrote, "The mass of men lead lives of quiet desperation." Failures don't know when to quit, but winners do. Failures believe that it is a disgrace to admit failure or to give up. Winners know how to minimize their losses and get out. It is okay to quit! It is okay to set another goal.

Step 4: Surround Yourself With Winners

One of the most powerful obstacles to a person's success is a lack of support. Constant and continuous exposure to negative recognition, criticism, belittling or resistance can destroy anybody's self-esteem. As a person with a purpose and direction, it is your responsibility to surround yourself with people who will support your best interests. As the saying goes, "Do not cast pearls before swine." Do not invest all your energy in trying to change a negative environment or person. Always be ready to take yourself out of it.

Winners are never alone unless they want to be. Choosing to live life on your own terms does not mean you are choosing to be a hermit. Granted, as you grow you may suffer, for there is little growth without conflict. You may leave some people behind. You may be judged harshly and feel the sting of opposition. But there will always be stimulating, exciting, supportive, results-oriented people there for you if you learn where to look.

A little girl wanted to ride her bike over to her grandmother's early one morning. But once in the backyard she realized a storm had knocked a tree onto her bicycle the night before. With determination, the little girl struggled a full twenty minutes to free her bike with no success.

Then she gave up and just stood there, tired and discouraged. Then her mother, who had been watching from the kitchen window, came and stood by her side. "Did you use all your strength, dear?" she asked. "Yes, Mama," the little girl replied. "Well, honey, I don't think you did," her mother smiled. "What do you mean? I certainly did," moaned the child. "No, sweetheart," her mother whispered, reaching out and embracing her little girl, "you didn't use me!"

Learn where to look for support. Surround yourself with winners. They come in all shapes and sizes, ages and professions. They are doctors, bus drivers, mothers, clerks, secretaries and teachers. Winners can be found everywhere. They are different and yet quite the same. You will recognize them by the qualities they possess. Winners have dignity, self-respect, healthy self-esteem and a strong sense of purpose. They set goals and they keep their commitments.

Winners create a life for themselves in which they do what they want the best way they know how — and feel good about it.

And so can you.

Step #2
Network to Get Known

by Anne Boe

Picture yourself in a limousine.

Dressed in the height of fashion, you are seated comfortably in a sleek, plush town car quietly making its way through the heart of America's financial pulse point, Wall Street in New York. After a few moments, you are whisked to a waiting elevator inside the World Trade Center, and then escorted with your associates to the penthouse suite, an elegant and obscenely spacious room whose windows face north, providing you with a breathtaking view of the Manhattan skyline.

You are there to receive the highest accolade of your professional life — the chairmanship of a $700 billion communications, energy and technology corporation, flagship of the Fortune 500 and, by even the most casual reckoning, the greatest industrial enterprise in the world. And for you, the first woman in the company's history so honored, there's an additional personal high. You think about it later, after the speeches and the handshakes, after the call from the President, after the exquisite dinner with all of New York literally at your feet.

You reflect on your professional life, and what's happened to get you there. Then through the candlelight, you catch sight of something moving . . . a spider on the wall. You think a moment about the spider, and you laugh quietly to yourself. That little bug, after all, was the way you really got started.

* * *

If you enjoyed the previous little flight of total fantasy, consider that it need not be the far-fetched dream you might think it is. Take into consideration the fact that many of America's major movers and shakers — the top CEOs and executives in business, industry, government and the media — routinely use a concept, a technique and a process as complex as the boardrooms it's used in, and as simple as promising to "stay in touch." Consider, if you will, the idea of "networking."

Networking is the concept, technique and process of developing and nurturing career contacts within your field, in order to pursue your career objectives, or to help others do the same thing. It can be likened to the casting of a fisherman's net over the water . . . the linking of different interconnecting systems in nature . . . or the spinning of one or a series of webs by a spider. Networking is using what you have — *in the broadest and most expansive sense possible* — to get what you want.

For women in particular, networking is a vital process in the professional arena. Networking involves helping other women to become more effective in the business world. It's beating a system that, by accident or by design, isolates and confines women as they move in a male-dominated environment. It's asking for help when you need it, and offering help when you're asked. Mary Scott Welch describes networking as "getting together to get ahead."

The word "networking" is a contemporary corruption of an old word, "network." Webster's New World Dictionary describes a network as "a group, system, etc., of interconnected or cooperating individuals." And for many uses of the old word, the meaning couldn't be more accurate. The most common use of the word concerns the three major television networks. Across the country, hundreds of large and small television and radio stations combine, exchanging information and ideas on news, programming, entertainment and sports coverage. In the broad sense, each is interconnected, each is linked with the other, each forms a part of the whole.

Like the mammoth undertaking of a television network, you too can develop important, meaningful networks in your professional and personal life. Through discipline, your own imagination, and diligent use of resources — both the ones you know about and the ones you don't even know you have — networking can be a powerful part of your life, and can result in successes which you never dreamed possible.

An Acquired Skill

Perhaps the best way of illustrating the power of networking is with a concrete example. Here, in an excerpt from Pulitzer Prize-winning author David Halberstam's book, *The Powers That Be,* is a true-life example of a relentless networker:

He was the incandescent man. Phil Graham walked into a room and took it over, charming and seducing whomever he wished, men and women alike. No one in Washington could match him at it, not even, in the days before he became President, John F. Kennedy . . . No one, no politician could work a room the way he did. . . . He also had that rare ability to make almost everyone he dealt with feel for a brief few moments that he or she was the most important person in that room. In a city where most important people were hell-bent on proving that *they* were the most important people in the room, that was a priceless gift . . .

The man described above is Philip L. Graham, the late publisher of *Newsweek* magazine and *The Washington Post,* in a social setting common to the heady, rarefied air of Washington, D.C. Graham's strategy fits networking to a T.

In American journalism, Graham is credited with helping to steer *The Post* from its former status as an erratic, inconsistent newspaper in the nation's capital to a first-rank product of international stature, a paper whose reporters later disclosed unprecedented corruption in the Watergate scandal.

But even with the impressive voice of *The Washington Post,* publisher Graham used his natural talents as a born networker: "No one could work a room the way he did." Graham had a prodigious appetite for professional achievement, and knew how to cultivate important contacts on *The Post*'s behalf. Through contacts in Congress, his social connections throughout Washington and friendships cultivated over the years — captains of government and the media — Graham exploited his understanding of the interconnection of politics and the media, doing so to great professional advantage and immense personal wealth.

"All well and good," you say. "But I'm not Philip L. Graham. I'm a single career women of thirty-one who sees a future for herself in my present business, but who can't quite put all the pieces together."

Fair enough. There are few such "born networkers" as Philip Graham. Networking is an acquired skill. And networking can help you recognize the differences between the myths of being the Ultimate Career Woman ... and the harsh realities of the working world.

Many professional women realize the impossibilities of being some kind of Superwoman. They understand the difficulties in balancing — or trying to balance — the complex roles of executive, mate, mother, friend, money- and time-manager. They know how even attempting such a precarious balance can have adverse effects on their future because of the stress, loss of self-esteem, and diminished confidence in their abilities.

But we can reduce the negative factors of the professional world with effective use of the networking principle.

Why Network?

"Why bother to network? What's in it for me?" Fair questions. Simply answered: Networking makes the most sense for success within the context of your professional life.

In previous times in American history, professional women (what few of them there were) were less reliant on networking to achieve status in a given field for many longstanding societal reasons. For all its advances, society in the first half of the twentieth century rigidly defined sex roles. Women were accepted as the nurturers of society, the mothers and wives and nurses — and not as the competitors within society. Long-established social conventions fixed women in domestic or, at best, professionally servile positions. You could aspire to be a homemaker, with all the fine conveniences of modern technology at your disposal, but you were still looked upon as solely a homemaker. That, or they fitted you with your own typewriter and let you sink or swim in the secretarial pool.

But in the last twenty years all that's changed. Shifting demographics, a fundamental change in birth patterns and the work force, and growing attention to career opportunities by women have all combined to radically — and permanently — alter the face of American business.

And because of that, networking is an indispensable tool for success. Why network? Because there are too many contacts within your field to be made, too many advertisements to be considered, too many important people to be reached and courted, too many pivotal career moves to be considered and changed ... there is simply too much going on to go it alone — especially when *you don't have to*. The role of women in business is constantly in motion and changing. Mutuality needs to be a part of that evolving role. To make progress you can't just keep up. Real success means getting ahead, and getting ahead often means application of that now-famous adage: Sometimes It's Not What You Know, It's Who You Know.

So why network?
- For inside information.
- For advice and ideas.
- For leads and referrals.
- For moral support.
- For a talk in strictest confidence.
- For that jaw-dropping surprise: an insight you never considered before.

Three Categories

We've previously made some quick, thumbnail definitions of

networking. They're all valid, all accurate. But we'll elaborate further by dividing networking into three categories, which we'll use to better understand networking as both practice and philosophy.

We'll address networking as:

1) a concept
2) a process
3) a practical technique

Networking as Concept.

In his epochal 1967 book, *The Medium Is The Massage,* the late philosopher, social critic and communications theorist Marshall McLuhan advanced the idea that "the new electronic interdependence" of the satellite age had recreated the modern world as "a global village — a simultaneous happening." "We have become irrevocably involved with, and responsible for, each other," McLuhan writes, and he's correct. That's a theoretical expression of networking on a global scale.

There's a more dramatic, real-life example, one which emphatically demonstrates the power and force of networking.

In July 1985, singer Bob Geldof realized the fruition of a long-held dream: organizing a global telethon using the talents of a broad field of popular musicians to raise money for African famine relief. Geldof's idea — a vast global *network* of performers, organizers, volunteers and financial donors — was wildly successful. An estimated 1.5 billion people in some 10 countries watched the Live Aid Concerts for Famine Relief on satellite television (another excellent networking device, in this case) and contributed over $50 million to aid the victims of the most catastrophic drought and famine in this century. The Live Aid concerts gave more credence to McLuhan's theory of the global village. Geldof's concerts made the whole world a village where — unencumbered by red tape and the smug workings of conventional diplomacy — the tribal drums were heard, loud and clear.

It's not stretching the point to say that these are two excellent examples of networking at its boldest and most ambitious. In and of themselves, they have marginal parallels with business *per se.*

But when examined in the visionary and pioneering sense of networking, they explain networking as a concept better than just about anything else ... using what you have, in the broadest sense you can think of, in order to get what you want.

Networking as Process.

Princess Jackson Smith, public information officer for the Washington State Department of Licensing, explained her perception of networking as an all-involving process:

> ... Networking is a natural human function. Each one of us has a network that helps us function in daily life — doctors, lawyers, mechanics, church associates, community organizations, colleagues. Networking is how you bought that new home or that new sofa that was on sale or that new car ...

That's one way to assess networking as a process. It could also begin with a cataloging, mental or otherwise, of the people needed to attain a certain professional level. The average professional comes into contact with hundreds of people in a given year, people who could be called upon to help advance that professional's career, and she could do the same for other professionals.

Networking as a process also entails an understanding of oneself as an interactive tool. Consider the drawing below in relation to you and your ability to network effectively.

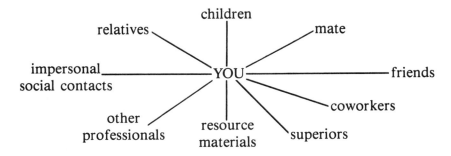

"YOU" are at the center of this conceptual model, at its heart and core. There's a good reason for this. YOU are the source of your own aspirations, your own desires and dreams. No one else dreams your dreams for you, no one assumes your aspirations for you. Your own career intentions are the single most powerful self-directing force you have at your disposal. Those intentions can be the catalyst for your networking efforts.

Notice the rays emanating from YOU in the diagram. These are some of the resources you can draw upon in your encounters with the networking principle. Consider each of them for a moment:

- Your coworkers. Those workers around you, those people on more or less an equal footing with respect to authority and position — your professional peers.
- Your superiors. These are coworkers in management or supervisory roles, people with a different vantage point of your job and your company.
- Your friends. These can be chums of long standing, the people you've grown up with and have come to trust and understand.
- Your mate. If you are married, this can be an invaluable ally, a person able to combine some friendly advice with information from his professional perspective — and able to offer the special and singular affection only a mate can provide. If you're not married, networking may even help you in that arena (more on this later).
- Your children. If you have kids, your children can be a wonderful source of news and information, depending on where they live and work and whom they know. Even if they're small children, they're a great source of inspiration and constant love.
- Your relatives. Your parents and grandparents can be another powerful source of information and referral. Having been out in the world longer than you, they know more, their circle of acquaintances is wider. They could be that wellspring of information you never thought you had.
- Impersonal social contacts. You know them: people you see on occasion. Sometimes, you might not quite remember who they are. There's cordiality between you, but you're not really friends yet. That's OK. Use the casual diffidence between you to your advantage. Drop names and try some pointed

small talk. Sometimes, you may learn more from a casual acquaintance who happens to be in the right place at the right time. You might even learn a lot.
- Other professionals. People in different fields than yours nonetheless hear and read about things that could be important to you. Stay in touch with people in allied fields. That way, you're covering bases for both your profession and another one that might be more attractive in the future.
- Resource materials. Materials found in libraries, bookstores, government offices and elsewhere can be a veritable gold mine of information — and a vital link in your attempts at effective networking.

Information has become the most fluid commodity there is. Nothing moves more quickly, and in such wide and random patterns of dispersal, as does information. Water may seek its own level, but information has no level, recognizes no limits to its ability to flow. It is the modern world's self-creating commodity, the abstract liquid of our age. And the progress of business depends on it.

Networking as process requires an understanding of the ubiquitous nature of information, and a knowledge of how YOU fit in the flow of that information. Networking as process employs the self as the center of the networking principle, from which all dreams and aspirations come. Networking as process means using the variety of resources available, with YOU choosing the ones that work best in your case. It means using the foregoing diagram as a model, a model of professional radial symmetry ... symmetry moving outward from the center ... come to think of it, the same symmetry as that which a spider uses to build a web.

Networking as Practical Technique.

Networking described as both concept and process should give you clues on how to implement networking as a practical, hands-on technique to your own advantage. We understand that McLuhan's idea of a vast interdependence is native to the networking *concept*. We also understand that there's a radial philosophy behind the *process* of networking. By combining elements of the two, it's clear that the raw materials for successful networking are already in place.

Networking practically means following through on your stated intentions, and using any device — technological, emotional, and conversational — to achieve your intentions. Tools you can use (though by no means is this a list of all of them) include the following:

- Letters.
- Calling on the telephone.
- Word-of-mouth.
- Books and other printed matter.

With just these four tools, we're using virtually all of the devices important to modern communication — and with one exception, the same tools of communication that have helped to inform and enrich the human family for hundreds of years. Let's briefly examine each.

One of the continually effective networking tools is the business letter. When precisely and cordially written, the business letter begins the networking principle properly, with a sharp and cogent introduction of yourself and your abilities. Consider some variations on the letter theme:

- Letters to other professionals outside your field.
- Letters to professionals within your field.
- Letters to contacts made through an introduction by friends or coworkers.
- Letters to prospective employers.
- Letters from your friends, superiors or coworkers to prospective employers on your behalf.
- Resume cover letters.

The telephone is equally effective, perhaps the most effective of the tangible communications tools at reach every day. With its worldwide voice and constant reliability, the telephone can quickly lay the introductory groundwork for an effective network.

Use of word-of-mouth as a networking tool is trickier than the others. It relies on accuracy and good judgment for its ability to work — and that's why it sometimes doesn't.

We've all heard the joke about how a message at one end of

a line of people starts one way and ends up something completely different. That's how the message "Joe has brown shoes and a blue tie" might become "Josephina has blue boots and a lavender tie" twenty people later. Spreading details about yourself via word-of-mouth should be done using only the sparest details. Learn how much information about yourself is too much. If you talk yourself up to another professional or a random social contact, using too much detail about your aspirations and strategies, you're only inviting yourself to be second-guessed. Disclosing too much about your intentions only confuses other people about you and complicates their evaluation of you.

And too much self-advertisement also robs you of the element that is indispensable to making a network work: the element of diplomatic secrecy, the confidentiality you need to help you nurture your plans where they grow best — in the dark.

When using word-of-mouth, broadcast just enough information about yourself to pique interest in yourself and your abilities. Be specific, but not *too* specific. Develop your network as a way of transmitting certain information about yourself — but not all the information. Keep them guessing about you. If it's done with the right touch, you'll notice that you will keep them interested in you as well.

The fourth primary tool for networking — printed matter — is of course readily available. Books, magazines, newspapers and other materials can be of enormous value. Many professionals limit themselves and their growth by inadequately drawing on this almost-limitless resource. There are, of course, the usual sources of information:

- Books and magazines.
- Newspapers.
- Pamphlets and press releases.

But there are many others. As you begin your network, consider:

- Professional quarterlies and periodicals.
- Statistical abstracts.
- Who's Who in the World, in America, and in separate regions of the U.S.
- Congressional Quarterly.

- Industry publications pertinent to the field you're interested in.
- Standard & Poor's Corporation Records.
- Fortune 500 and Fortune 1000 listings.
- Court transcripts.
- Records on microfilm and microfiche.
- Theses and dissertations.
- Employee and corporate directories.

The possibilities are almost endless, even if the list isn't. Your library reference room is a storehouse of information which you can use in your networking efforts to great advantage.

Remember, too, that the networking principle is not one forced to rely solely on living, breathing beings in order to function. Networking isn't just with people; it often means finding pertinent information that you require. Networking means linking up with knowledge as well as with people in order to realize your professional objective.

Internal Networking

Successful practical networking requires discipline and attention to some order or procedure that works for you. Networking isn't just plugging into outlets of information and advice. On a new job, it's sticking to your objectives during a high-pressure time.

Starting a new job is never easy, and always challenging. It's vital to begin networking internally, within the workplace, in order to know who's in the power positions and correctly assess the communications patterns at work in the eternal office grapevine. Who's in? Who's out? Who's flexing their muscles? Who's working behind the scenes? Careful and consistent internal networking can get you the best seat in the house for the dramas of the workplace.

Even in your current job, internal networking can mean the difference between successful advancement and standing in place. Observe the employees who have arrived since you started there, the ones who are going places . . . the ones who get their own offices in an incredibly short time. The chances are excellent that the networking principle is at work for them.

There are other ways of networking in the workplace, not necessarily in the broad scale we've discussed earlier, but on an intra-company level that can help place you in a stronger, more advantageous position.

• Decide on your role in the workplace, articulate an image in your dress, manner, and your vocal style. Then portray these personal characteristics consistently.

• Speak to everyone. No matter what you've heard about successful people conversing mainly with those cloistered in "the halls of power and wealth," don't pick and choose selectively. Everyone in your work environment is important; everyone is a potential link in the network.

• Be courteous. Don't be stingy with the word "thanks," and use it in writing if the situation calls for it. Minding your manners gets you noticed.

• Be concise and articulate. In your memos and conversations, develop a talent for brevity. This will go a long way toward establishing you as a dynamic communicator . . . and isn't communication what networking is really all about?

• Extend yourself. Be willing now and then to put yourself out, to do someone a favor when the opportunity arises. By doing favors for others, you're ensuring reciprocal treatment when you need a hand.

• Make yourself approachable. Develop an attitude of openness and friendliness in your encounters with other workers. It makes people more receptive to the idea of sharing information and ideas — of networking — with YOU.

• Learn the subtleties of small talk. Contrary to some opinions, there is no easy mastery of small talk, especially now, in an age in which spontaneous talk is giving way to more directed, electronically-contrived formats of conversing. But you can feel comfortable in the art of chitchat. There are many relaxation and self-programming aids available that help in defusing the nervous, "scattered" feeling many professionals experience when forced to speak off the cuff. Or when placed in very tight situations, such as when ten minutes of small talk with the CEO of Exxon just can't be avoided in a stuck elevator.

There are many different approaches to succeeding in the art of small talk. It's safe to say that a common thread to all of them is to relax and be yourself. Don't waste energy building a contrivance, pretending to be someone you're not. Start with an introduction and an innocent comment that invites a reaction. Listen, interact ... and oh yes, have fun! Small talk is that facet of career life that can be both professionally enlightening and a heck of a good time — if you let it be.

Other Tools

In addition to the foregoing techniques, you'll also need other, secondary tools of the networking principle, tangible items to help you in developing the organizational side of networking.

One of the best tools is a personal resource center, which might be any address and phone book. But for the best system, find a book, binder or notebook made of more durable stuff, preferably leather. (Leather's always a class touch, anyway.) Your system should include both current and future calendars, addresses, phone numbers, a listing of your prospective networkees, a listing of professional organizations, an appointment book and an ample supply of your business cards. Somewhere, too, you might include a short list of important birthdays ... yes, birthdays. It never hurts someone's career to remember the boss' natal day.

Successful networkers often adhere to other guidelines as well:

Report back to anyone who gives you a lead. That keeps you a vital link in your own network, and indicates interest to your other links.

As you progress professionally, stay in touch with your old links in the network. Call them sometime, out of the blue, just to chat, or write a letter. Remember that success hinges on constant, relentless exchanging of information. The same contacts you ignore or forget on your way up you may have to deal with again — on your way down.

Deliver on your promises. If your word's no good, what good is your network? Without following through on your promises and your commitment, your network won't expand very far. Once word gets around, you might be the only person in it.

Include a wide variety of people of different backgrounds and ages. It stands to reason that the wider your network — the fewer people you're willing to exclude — the more profitable your results will probably be.

Don't tell everything to everybody. Again, one of the most important elements of successful networking is maintaining diplomatic secrecy — knowing when to tell something, knowing who to tell it to and knowing how to say it right. The best-laid plans of mice and networkers oft go awry because of an untimely disclosure.

Don't be discouraged if someone doesn't want to develop a network with you. Not everyone is as open-minded and forward-thinking as you are. Accept that fact, and get on with the business of networking with the people who know a good thing when they see one.

Don't expect an instant answer. Just as it takes time to put through a transcontinental phone call or respond to a letter, networking takes time. I equate networking with the planting of a garden. You are constantly planting seeds when networking. Just like with a garden, you never know when the seeds are going to come up. Dealing with people in the networking process is the same way. You never know when that little kernel of information will result in something breaking through the soil, bearing fruit for you. Be patient.

Other Advantages

Besides the ones we've already cataloged, networking has other important functions, peripheral functions that are a basic part of every networking effort — functions that are benefits as well.

1. Networking as Infinitely Expanding.

The previous diagram pictured YOU as the center of the conceptual model. Now expand on that diagram. Consider that all of your contacts — friends, relatives, coworkers, other professionals — all have contacts of their own, people they know who may be in a position to help. In addition, those people know other people who know other people who know . . . you get the idea. In this way, networking is a theoretically infinite, constantly expanding principle. If you had the time to do it, you could follow your initial contacts indefinitely. You can see how a little diligent networking effort can go a long way.

2. Networking as Source of Solace.

Networking is also a marvelous method of combating the isolation and alienation that often occur among women professionals. Face it: as a professional woman, you are one of a small handful of businesspeople whose drive and determination are moving you to the top. That can unfortunately have the effect of shutting you off from other workers — some of whom may have been your close friends not long ago. You feel isolated from your past, partly because you're moving away from it. You're leaving comfortable territory behind, heading out into uncharted waters. For even the most ardent and committed professional, that can be a scary experience.

Networking enables you to make and cultivate contacts of other like-minded people, people who share your ambition and your feelings of isolation. Networking can be a way to find solace, camaraderie and a friendly shoulder to lean on. This can lead to another kind of networking.

Personal Networking

Who says networking stops when you walk out the office door at 5 p.m.? Effectively used, networking can help you in your personal life . . . in meeting possible romantic interests . . . in fighting the emotional desolation that is often a consequence of life in the non-stop, upwardly mobile 80s.

Dedication to your profession can have a harmful effect on your personal life. You have only so many hours in the day, and when a large part of your time is devoted to professional advancement, there's naturally less time to cultivate the other important facets of your life. The pace of your life won't get any less hectic as you rise on the ladder, that's for sure. So, one effective way to develop your emotional side is by using the same tools you're using to develop your professional side.

Personal networking isn't quite as involved as professional networking. It necessarily relies on a tight and reliable circle of friends, people you can turn to for companionship at parties, meetings, shows and concerts . . . people who can coax you out of the hand-tailored shell you might find yourself in. With personal networking, your friends and relatives will be a solid resource.

If you're in a new job, a good means of internal/personal networking is with one person whom you suspect you might be compatible. Find out about the night life in your new locale, "what's happening" after dark. If you're receptive and friendly, you'll open a door on a new friendship — one link in your new network — and discover where the social action lurks after hours.

For personal networking to succeed, you have to again follow certain disciplines. First, you'll have to take initiative. Other workers may or may not notice the new wallflower in Data Processing, the mousey young woman who works the regulation eight hours and goes home. You'll have to make the first step. Announce yourself, let them know you're around. Visibility is key to effective personal networking. So is a healthy dose of aggressiveness.

Since your professional networkees certainly won't all be women, you've got a leg up on making those romantic encounters happen. (Be advised, though, office romances can be a risky endeavor. The availability factor is nice, but unfortunately, they can complicate life in the workplace in many different ways.)

The special networking nuances of women can work to your advantage. Women tend to be more in contact with their emotional makeup. This doesn't mean we're more susceptible to "flying off the handle," as the male-created stereotype would have us believe. It means that women weigh their emotions and "gut feelings" more carefully in the context of personal interaction.

Also, women still aren't that common in American business. It's a geometric progression that's regrettable but true: the higher up the corporate ladder you go, the fewer women there are around you.

And don't be afraid to use the pertinent machinery of networking for your personal life. Networking is but a different way of saying "the old-boy system," the legitimate grandfather to the networking principle. And there's nothing that says it can't be a "new-girl system" too.

Going For It: The Spider-Web Effect

We've discussed networking in a variety of ways, but it's up to you to use the techniques here to your best advantage. Perhaps not every one will work for you, but most of them will. Use them regularly and confidently. You'll see the difference effective networking can make in your life.

And don't forget the spider. Using the "spider-web effect" — with YOU at the center, enlarging your professional and personal range by using *all* of the resources at your disposal — can yield surprising dividends in your life. Networking can keep you at your peak every business day, and after every business day. It can mean a matrix of loyal, caring, sympathetic friends and associates who can make your climb to satisfaction a rewarding one.

Networking can be a solid cornerstone on which to build your life.

And who knows? It just might get you a ride in a limousine, too.

Step #3
Project
A High
Profile

---

by Lee Milteer

It's time to think about advertising the most important product you'll ever come across: you.

In the simplest definition possible, advertising is printed or spoken matter that calls attention to items for sale or otherwise available for public consideration. In the earliest days of advertising, goods for sale were pretty much the basics: flour, oil, machinery, livestock, ammunition. But as American society advanced and grew more sophisticated, and as our economic base continued its shift from an agricultural emphasis to an industrial one, advertising grew in its sophistication as well. A broader range of products was advertised and geared to a more educated and cautious consumer clientele. Today's ads for automobiles, personal computers and leisure technology demonstrate how modern advertising has kept pace with modern demands.

As a professional you, too, are a product. Think about how

advertising might help your life, and you'll see how self-salesmanship can help you. You'll understand how the same principles of advertising, once applied strictly to inanimate goods and services, now carry over into human resources. Consider then the benefits of self-promotion and self-projection — advertisements for YOURSELF.

With other chapters of this book, you've learned that success is achieved step by step. It's the methodical, incremental approach to achieving your objectives that yields profitable results. You've also learned some different and refreshing strategies with which to achieve those objectives. In this chapter, we'll explore aspects of the self-promotional process: your self-image; how old thoughts and closeted quirks undercut your drive; how to be remembered; "packaging" your strengths convincingly, and several techniques for implementing self-promotion and cultivating your self-confidence.

Many key elements must come into focus for you to be the person you want to be. The sharper your self-image and the more unshakable your self-confidence, the more powerful you will appear to the outside world. Let's start by looking at one real-life example...

I. The Farmer's Daughter

From the start, I knew I was going to be different.

Don't ask me how. I sensed deeply that I would work to get the kind of freedom I saw given to boys when I was young. Boys were given a "blank check" to chart the direction of their lives. I wanted the same. But how could I get it? I was a farmer's daughter, growing up in an isolated, rural part of Virginia. I had only the most standard and traditional of female role models. All of the women I knew worked only in their homes. These women had no real understanding of how to nurture confidence or to reach success in the outside world. Generally, most of them looked to their strong, wise husbands to deal with people from outside the home.

Of course, I was expected to follow suit, to remain in the proverbial "woman's place." But I sensed I could break out of that mold. When very young, I was a tomboy, and I thought it unfair that girls were given one direction in life to explore while boys got another. I wanted to be myself, and not to abide by the old rules.

By the time I was in my early teens, my desires became even clearer. I didn't want to go through life following other people's tired expectations. I became aware of the fact that women were (and still are) programmed from birth to trust someone else's opinions and judgments, rather than making their own. Without realizing it then, I was writing the beginning part of the script for an advertisement for myself. I was bolstering my belief that I was UNIQUE.

To be truly successful, you must always remind yourself that you are unique. You must identify your own style and personality. Give people an indelible imprint of you. We've all had different social, economic and educational environments that helped shape our personalities. But a common denominator exists for all truly successful people, no matter what their backgrounds: each one develops and nurtures a strong self-image.

You'll find plenty of evidence supporting factors such as economic level or ethnic status as the prime determinants of success. But new evidence suggests that the major factor in determining success is plain and simple: self-image.

The question, "How can I be more successful in life?" might just as well be, "What can I do to enhance my self-image?"

In my early twenties, I discovered a book that made a lot of sense to me — *Psychocybernetics,* by Dr. Maxwell Maltz. It gave me the blueprint with which to develop a positive self-image. Among the novel concepts in Maltz's book was a classic example of the importance of self-image.

As a plastic surgeon, Dr. Maltz performed a broad range of cosmetic surgeries to correct his patients' perceptions of unattractive physical features, such as a nose too big or a deformity suffered in an accident. Maltz discovered, however, that many patients' post-operative self-image was just as bad as it was before surgery. In other words, if patients felt unattractive before surgery, they still saw themselves as unattractive when the bandages were unwrapped and they looked in the mirror. Maltz contended, and I agree, that we do not see exclusively with our eyes. More importantly, we see with our brains. The picture we see when we look in the mirror is the picture of ourselves buried deep in our subconscious.

II. Visualization and Mental Programming:
A Matter of Attitude

That's how we limit ourselves. Based on what other people have told us, we have programmed negative things into our subconscious. We have formed opinions or pictures in our subconscious of ourselves, our abilities, and our potential in life. To fully realize our potential, or to change the picture we project to others, it's necessary to change the self-image we carry in our subconscious.

If you have recorded negative attitudes about your abilities or potential, then you have contributed to the formation of a negative self-image. You will be stuck with these self-limiting opinions of yourself until you deliberately convert them to a more realistic and self-confident view.

Consider your past.

What psychological baggage were you saddled with when you were young — the old myths about what is "masculine" and "feminine"? Do you remember the old saws: how little girls were "sugar and spice and everything nice," how they aren't good at math "because they don't have scientific minds," how "nice girls don't get angry and aren't pushy," and how girls should wait for "Prince Charming to come along and rescue them so they don't have to worry about a career"? Think about how these messages affected you and your beliefs about reality. How are they adversely influencing your self-image even now?

One thing I did to help construct a more positive self-image after reading Dr. Maltz's book was to *continue* reading, especially anything I could find about famous women. I learned that most of them were successful because they chose to develop their potential on their own terms, whether society liked it or not. This helped me when forming my success strategies because I began to realize that, inevitably, some people would not approve of my actions. Comparing my personal quest with those of famous women helped me to realize that it was totally up to me to make myself into what I wanted to become.

I started to review in my mind some of the decisions I had made about my potential from the beginning of my life. I had always been a poor speller, but when I reviewed why, I found that a childhood experience had been the genesis of my lack of spelling confidence. When I was in fourth grade, I came home from school one day with a dispiriting F in spelling on my report card. I was an average student, usually making Bs or Cs. I knew my mother would put me on some kind of restriction because of that F, so I did what any smart fourth-grader would do...every chore my mother usually had to yell to get me to do.

I cleaned up my room. I washed the dishes. I dusted and straightened things. I even took out the trash.

My mother, a smart woman, knew right away that something was up. She called me into the kitchen and said, "Lee, either you've done something very bad, or...it's report card day." Clearly outfoxed by a superior force, I sighed and handed her my report card. She looked at the F and said, "Well, I guess I should be mad at you for failing your spelling class, but I can't because I can't spell either."

A light bulb went on in my head. "No wonder I can't spell," I thought. "I must have defective spelling genes. Mom can't spell, so it must run in the family." From then on, I never tried to learn to spell. I figured that if Mom couldn't be a good speller, neither could I. This demonstrates how I limited myself in one area, but there are hundreds of areas in which women limit themselves every day — by not reviewing and kicking out old, outdated beliefs about their potentials.

Some scientists theorize that we use as little as 10 percent of our natural abilities. That leaves up to 90 percent of our potential untouched. One way to tap into that potential is to study successful people and to develop new role models.

The best manual for studying successful people, in my opinion, is *Think and Grow Rich* by Napoleon Hill, written in the 1930s. The famous multimillionaire industrialist and philanthropist, Andrew Carnegie, commissioned Hill to perform a long-term study of successful people. Carnegie wanted to know why most people were average, while others improved themselves to become outstanding in their chosen fields of endeavor. What Hill found directly parallels our analysis of self-image: the difference between a successful person and an average one is not social standing, education or IQ, but *motivation* — a symbiotic factor in developing a positive self-image. Hill distilled information from many different, successful sources. In doing so, he came up with some techniques for attaining success.

The first technique was understanding that successful people have a positive mental attitude. They believe in themselves, have faith in their abilities — even when they fail.

The second technique Hill emphasized was the use of visualization, which is a different way of saying the use of the imagination, that "workshop of the mind." Hill asserted that anything you can create in your mind, you can accomplish: "Whatever the mind of man can conceive and believe, it can achieve."

To explain visualization, you must first understand that it is a tool for self-programming. Your brain resembles a computer in a number of ways. It's your job to "program" yourself mentally in order for your desires to become reality. You might have heard the phrase common to the computer industry: "Garbage In, Garbage Out." This same principle is true of your mind. Whatever you put into it — your internal language, self-evaluation, your motivation — imprints on your subconscious. If you find yourself constantly surrounded by negative people with negative ideas, the results can be damaging to your future success.

One example of this is in one's response to the greeting "How are you?" When faced with such a greeting, many people feel compelled to reply "fine," or worse yet, they say "all right" or "fair to middling." Imagine the long-term effect this type of a "garbage" response has on your subconscious and your self-image. Why not program yourself to be "great" or "terrific" or "better than ever"? Remember: every day, and in ways far simpler than you might imagine, you are continuously creating your self-concept — and therefore, defining your own potential.

Henry Ford has been credited with a remark that dates from the turn of the century, yet still has contemporary applications: "If you think you can or if you think you cannot, you are always right."

With your thoughts, your ideas and your vision of yourself in the world, you program yourself for success or failure.

This is why visualization is so important. To use visualization, you imprint positive new programs into your computer (your brain), and keep out those self-limiting thoughts. Don't put an unclear, garbled program into the computer and expect satisfactory results. Feed in instructions that are clear, vivid and to the point. Visualization is rehearsal for the future.

Having been in sales for some twelve years now, I've learned to feel very comfortable in a one-on-one sales presentation. But let me describe my first encounter with visualization. Back in 1978, I was to make a presentation to a group of investors considering the purchase of a shopping center. It was a large center, so an equally large commission was involved. I was so terrified at the prospect of standing in front of those 20 or so people, I almost turned down the opportunity.

Do you know that public speaking is the Number One Fear of business people? Ahead of death, snakes and root canal work! People would rather endure physical pain — or die outright — than speak in public. And I felt the same way. But I knew I had to counter the dread that filled me.

So I read *Think and Grow Rich* once more and I told myself the effort would be worth it. The commission, after all, was a great deal of money, and I certainly was interested in that.

I also began to visualize. Each day upon waking, I made a conscious effort to remain relaxed, calm. I would see myself standing in front of those 20 people, confident and well-prepared. What I projected in my imagination, and what I repeated tirelessly to myself, was a picture, a vision of myself standing in front of those people, hearing them applauding the power and clarity of my presentation, and then seeing them signing the contract. All I did for the three weeks before the presentation was play and replay this mental movie about the person I was going to become. Gradually, my fear began to subside.

When the day of the acid test arrived and I actually made the speech, I was nervous for the first few minutes. But then, in much the same way other salespeople go into an "automatic mode" after the first of their speech, I lost my nervousness. The results I had envisioned in my mind's eye were starting to happen in real life. The people applauded, thanked me and signed the contract a week later.

I had successfully rehearsed for success and success happened.

We can do this in virtually any situation. If you're nervous when you meet a client for the first time or you do something you've never done, *imagine* the successful conclusion of the task. Then fill in the details. Flesh it out, make it as real as a fantasy can be. Envision yourself handling all the objections to your ideas. In your mind's eye, witness the business prospect signing the contract and benefiting from the transaction. Then, visualize yourself returning to your office to the effusive praise of your boss (who invites you into her office for something from the wet bar and a chat about "your future with the company"). See yourself enjoying life more fully with the extra money success can bring.

But even such a dramatic and powerful tool as visualization cannot work miracles. Changes in you and in your attitude won't develop overnight. Your aspirations and your strategies for achieving them must be part of a gradual process. So, whatever objectives you choose, start off small. If I'd said to myself that I was going to stand up in front of 200 people at the start of my career, I wouldn't have taken the opportunity. I wouldn't have been comfortable with even trying to step before such a large crowd. So I started with 20. Then came a group of 30, then 50, then 100. From there, of course, it was up, up and away. I recently spoke at an AT&T meeting in New Jersey before a tight, friendly little crowd of 800 people. It was a wonderful experience — one I was able to enjoy because of a gradual approach to public speaking.

There's something to be said for making progress in increments — whether it's public speaking or even dieting. Dieters often set their initial goals based on the beautiful models we see in magazines and on TV. Then, of course, the dieters feel awful when they can't quickly shed 20 pounds and look like Ms. Cosmopolitan! A more productive, less frustrating method might be to see themselves on a scale weighing 137 pounds instead of 140...then, weighing 132 instead of 137...then 128 instead of 132. Don't try to change too swiftly, or "go for all the marbles at once." Instead, adopt a well-paced, orderly approach to personal changes. Changes should be gradual. The meaningful changes — the ones that stay with you — usually are.

III. Rehearsal

Now let's discuss the dynamics of self-confidence and visualization; that is, ways to make them work.

In 1984 I presented a workshop for a large, prestigious *Fortune 500* company in New York. At lunch I had the opportunity to speak with one of the firm's vice presidents. Eventually, after some peripheral conversation, we got around to discussing how important it is to look self-confident in the business world.

This VP looked at me and smiled. "Lee, do you know how I make myself look brilliant?" I wasn't sure if he was kidding or serious. But he was in earnest. He told me how he handled himself in business situations such as presenting a new idea for consideration, lobbying for a heftier budget or even selling a new product to his staff. The secret, he said, was in giving the impression of just having thought of the idea. "What looks like talking off the cuff is really a well-thought-out and prepared presentation."

Like an actor reading his lines, this vice president has all of his major ideas together long before the meeting. And like an actor, he knows that the delivery of his lines is a matter of good timing — and that good timing is often just as important as the idea itself.

The vice president said he always makes a point of outlining his ideas on paper — organized and concise. Then he writes them out longhand, combining his facts, doing research and rehearsing his "impromptu" speech with his wife for her criticism and suggestions. He even takes the rehearsal phase a step further by standing in front of the mirror to include the right mannerisms. He then turns on a tape recorder, so he can review the material as it was spoken.

Finally, the vice president said he records himself with a video-cassette recorder and looks at the videotape 24 hours later to review both the material and his presentation skills. This gives him the clearest possible picture of his strengths and weaknesses.

"Whew!" I said. "That's a lot of work."

"Don't I know it," he replied. "But it's the hard work that gets you ahead. It's the extra edge that you have over your coworkers that makes you move up faster. Being an average presenter would have kept me in the pack."

With such dividends potentially yours, can you afford not to rehearse for your future?

IV. The Billboard

Now let's explore some suggestions for promoting yourself toward success.

Let's say you have learned or are learning to project self-confidence, even though you still feel the occasional rush of butterflies. You're working in a career you find exciting and challenging. How do you move ahead?

To be successful in today's competitive world, you need more than the right background, the right college degree and knowing the right people. To get ahead, it's also important to promote yourself within your community and profession. If you don't have vocal, publicized confidence in yourself, who can react to you? If you're unwilling to promote yourself, who will? Learn to incorporate your personal strengths into every facet of your visual self-image.

Think of yourself as a billboard, advertising your New! and Improved!ness.

Whether self-employed or part of an established firm, learning to promote yourself is a necessary part of life — particularly for women.

Our educational system and our society didn't teach us how to promote ourselves for success. Instead, we have learned to be modest about our own accomplishments, reluctant to brandish our achievements. With the exception of what happens in modern sports, few "pep" rallies are ever held to promote individuals. (Japanese industrial management, with its growing attention to worker participation and on-the-job enthusiasm, might be starting to change that, but none too quickly.) Instead, we are taught to wait for others to notice our achievements, as if our gifts were a cache of treasures waiting to be discovered and unearthed only by others.

However, in this area of self-promotion changes are coming. More people are aware that success is determined by how self-confident the individual feels and how one communicates that self-confidence to the business world. Read the daily newspaper. You'll read about the comers, the professionals who once were gun-shy about self-promotion, but who now are more vocal and visible about their abilities. Our society still holds tenaciously to the Puritan ethic, but even that is beginning to change; it's more acceptable today to actively seek recognition for work. And the new self-promoters aren't a bit reticent to tell the world about their products and services.

People prefer to associate with winners. People who promote themselves tactfully and confidently look like winners.

An important way to get people to perceive you as a cut above the average is with personal public relations — personal PR.

Consider your appearance.

Personal appearance is important for good personal PR. When a person's look becomes outdated or is too flashy or ostentatious, people often assume that the person might also have outdated ideas, or could be too brash and noisy to be an effective, diplomatic communicator. Your outward appearance is a mirror of the professional you. Don't take chances.

Go to the experts to make sure you look the way you want to appear, from your hair down to your shoes. Go to a professional image consultant. Have a professional assess your hairstyle, makeup, eyeglasses, clothes and footwear. As you plan your program of personal promotion, don't overlook the impact of your appearance.

Consider your visibility.

It's important to develop visibility within your professional field. Join professional groups and organizations. But don't just be another name on a long membership list — get involved! Join an internal committee, then set a goal of becoming an officer of the group. Besides the obvious merits of promoting yourself, you will quickly realize satisfaction in giving something of yourself to others.

Once you make contact with those outside your immediate circle of friends and acquaintances, you will find it necessary to know how to introduce yourself. Again, the self-deprecating ethic hammered into us in our youth might rear its ugly head. Often people will introduce themselves by giving only their names, even in professional settings. But surely you are more than a name.

In my "Image & Self-Projection" seminar I teach "The 33-Second Intro," something every professional should know. Many behaviorists and employers believe that a solid impression of a person is often made in less than 33 seconds. Thus, the 33-Second Intro is a way of creating a "commercial" starring yourself. The point is to leave a memorable, polished impression of yourself on new contacts.

Think of all the things you can say about yourself in 33 seconds. What do you do? Where do you work and live? Is the nature of your business easily understood from its name or is more explanation necessary?

I prefer an introduction like this: "I am a professional speaker and trainer and now annually present 85 public seminars called 'Image and Self-Projection' throughout the southeastern United States. I also produce and host a popular cable television show called 'Lifestyles,' which airs in metropolitan Virginia."

Say that to yourself. When you make your own introduction, keep it just about this short, then practice making it sound natural. Concise, informative and all done in less than a minute. Notice that I used only "facts" — no bragging or boasting in my commercial. Always remember to leave people with the most positive impression of yourself.

You'll want to do other things when you introduce yourself to demonstrate self-confidence and a willingness to make contact with the other person. A strong, firm handshake is one, especially if you are a woman. Women have been characterized far too long as "the weaker sex." While you're shaking hands with your right hand, your left hand should be reaching into your pocket for that most effective promotional tool: the business card. Visual reinforcement of the verbal message will ensure that you stay in the other person's mind. Direct eye contact, a ready smile and a genuine willingness to listen to the other person — these complete the steps of a first-class introduction.

Next on the list of self-promotion techniques is attending trade shows, business fairs and other large-scale events that will improve you professionally and give you the benefit of public exposure. Schedule your time so you can attend events that attract the leaders of your business or profession. To be seen and associated with successful people enhances your own professional image.

Get involved in local events, as well. The local Chamber of Commerce is an excellent place to start.

For women especially, joining one of the many women's networking groups which have sprung up across the country in recent years can have an important effect on a career. Business and professional women have become increasingly aware of the inequalities in the business world. They are ready and willing to provide mutual support services such as work against job discrimination, help in achieving equal pay for equal work and advice on a wide variety of subjects from daycare to job-sharing. Professional women realize that their counterparts throughout history traditionally have filled roles in which they were taught to compete with one another and vie for the attention of men. Men, on the other hand, learned to work together, to "become a team." The need for women to learn these aspects of cooperation in the business world is acute. Many organizations exist for professional women and are good sources for networking information. See Step #2 on "Networking" for more insight into this process.

It seems that in every office there's at least one woman who always arrives at work on time and leaves late, works quietly at her desk all day, seldom takes a break and never takes personal leave. In the same office, there's a guy on the same job level who arrives late to work, leaves early and seems to spend the rest of his time at the water cooler telling everyone within earshot his latest great idea. When promotion time rolls around, who gets it? The woman? No, the man by the water cooler. Why? Partly, at least, because he's learned the art of self-promotion.

Now, I'm certainly not saying you should slack off on your job in order to let people know your best points, but it is possible to do any number of innovative, creative things in order to become known around the office. For example, volunteer to present special training seminars or act as coordinator for an important event.

Estelle, a woman who attended my seminar in Norfolk, told me of her experiences working for a large corporation. She had the same education and background as several men at her job level and wanted to be promoted. Estelle offered to give up her lunch period one day a week in order to train other employees in her field. Six months later, she was the only one at her job level to be promoted. You can make it happen, too!

The Public Presentation: 12 Techniques

Try using a hobby for self-promotion. One amateur photographer I know offered to record special events for the company. She became visible by taking photos at the annual Christmas party and other activities. She made sure to take pictures of the bosses and after developing them would send a nice 5″ × 7″ print to those people, saying "I enjoyed the party" or "I thought you would like a copy of the picture I took." As an alternative to this approach, you might want to write articles or volunteer art for the company newsletter.

Start to speak and to ask questions at meetings. Begin discussions at workshops and conferences. Volunteer to research a project for the company. Before you do these things, review these pages on self-promotion. You might want to rehearse in front of a mirror or make an audio cassette or videotape. Here are some specific suggestions for making a solid impact at meetings when you speak:

(1) Be sure that if you intend to suggest an idea for a meeting, write it out and distribute copies as soon as you're finished speaking so it's clearly established as your contribution.

(2) Focus your attention on success and be positive about what you want to accomplish. Know that fear is normal — use that energy to project yourself into the audience.

(3) Think of your presentation as an adventure and enjoy it. Don't take everything so seriously. Humor and a positive attitude work wonders.

(4) Listen, as well as speak. Let your body language demon-

strate your interest. Sit straight, lean forward.

(5) Take several slow, deep breaths before you start to speak. This lowers your heartbeat so you will feel more in control.

(6) Use cue cards or an outline to refer to if you lose your train of thought while speaking. Don't read from notes for more than 60 seconds. Organize the key points. Use visuals whenever possible to hold the interest of your audience. A handout will visually reinforce your words.

(7) Make friends with your audience. Think of them as a group of dear friends instead of worrying about what they are thinking while you give your presentation. Make eye contact with as many people as possible. Find kind eyes and focus on people who are with you, not those who seem disinterested.

(8) Be enthusiastic. Try to get people to participate with you. Be animated.

(9) Use your voice to sound believable. Project with confidence.

(10) Try to anticipate negative questions so you can prepare a response. If no one responds to your idea or suggestion, repeat it from a different angle or point of view. Remember, we're the ones responsible for selling our ideas to others.

(11) End your presentation in your allowed time frame; it's better to end a few minutes early than to go overtime.

(12) After your presentation, look into your audience and smile. Acknowledge the applause and mentally pat yourself on the back.

The Press Release

Another important way to become known in your field is to send out press releases when you've done something newsworthy. Such items include promotions, awards or activities involving the public or a large group. Be sure to put together a first-class press release. A press package should include a biographical fact sheet, reprints of any significant publicity you have received in the past and formal black-and-white photographs at least 5″ × 7″ in size. An added feature might be copies of speeches you've given on the subject.

Here's a copy of a press release I issued; you might use it as a guide. Note the words "For Immediate Release" in the upper left-hand corner. Also, a contact name and number should be featured prominently in case the reporter wants to feature a more in-depth story.

Lee Milteer Associates
CAREER DEVELOPMENT STRATEGISTS

FOR IMMEDIATE RELEASE   Contact: Ann Smith
(804) 622-5599

**LEE MILTEER: BRINGING PRACTICAL EXPERIENCE
TO THE BUSINESS WORLD**

Lee Milteer does not believe in "ivory tower" training and motivation.

Instead, her training and motivation are based on the value of experience combined with creative problem-solving. It's proved to be a successful combination for her in the business world.

Lee Milteer has been a professional in sales and marketing for over 10 years. As vice president of a service business, she led the company from a small operation with only 100 accounts to over 1,200 accounts — an accomplishment that generated over a quarter million dollars a year in profit. She has taught university courses in sales and has lectured at many private seminars and classes for business and industry. Lee is now the president of her own consulting firm, and is the TV talk show host of *Lifestyles Magazine* in southeastern Virginia.

Lee Milteer is a member of the National Speakers Association, the American Society for Training and Development, and a director of the Southeastern Virginia Real Estate Educators Association.

P.O. BOX 11024 • NORFOLK, VIRGINIA 23517 • TELEPHONE (804) 622-5599

Send your press package to all newspapers in the community where you live and work. Also send it to the newsletters of professional, trade and civic organizations. And don't forget your alumni journals. You'll be amazed at the number of publications you can contact.

While you practice these self-promotion techniques, remember that other people you meet in the professional world are concerned with their visibility, no matter how secure they appear to be. People notice when someone else notices them. Pay attention to them when they talk — really pay attention! Compliment others on their accomplishments or even small personal touches such as a new suit. Remembering someone's name and where you met them is a great way to impress a person you've seen only once. Simple things such as sending birthday cards to bosses or clients improve your visibility: you took the time to care about someone else's special day.

Invest in yourself daily by reading self-help books, by visualizing success and by listening to motivational tapes to keep your attitude positive. Keep looking for the good in yourself and don't be afraid of showing it to the world. That's what professional savvy is all about — doing what you have to do to get ahead, working hard with an air of self-confidence and being visible to the right people at the right times.

Limits exist only in your mind.

Step #4
Communicate
With
Power

by Julie White

W hen you looked at Nell, the nursing coordinator of a major hospital in the Washington area, you saw a well-groomed, sophisticated professional woman. While I envied her for her height, Nell told me that as a gangly teenager in high school she had towered above the boys. To compensate for her feelings of awkwardness, Nell developed a corrective measure. She would hunch over, round her shoulders, cross her arms over her chest and lean against a wall whenever she felt nervous or uncomfortable.

As an adult, Nell was not aware that she continued to practice this behavior, and if you had asked her about it, she would have said she only reverted to this adolescent behavior when she felt shy. But Nell's subordinates at work got a very different impression. They saw their boss leaning arrogantly against the wall, scowling, her arms folded in front of her. What Nell felt was shyness, her employees saw as aloofness, arrogance and hostility.

Nell attended my seminar, then went back and asked a trusted subordinate to monitor her behavior and point out any way she might be sabotaging her power. She was surprised to hear that people often thought of her as aloof, hostile and arrogant. Instead of defending herself against these projected misconceptions, Nell knew that the meaning of her message was what other people perceived. Nell's subordinate gently reminded her whenever she fell back into her slumping pattern. After correcting her bearing to one of confidence, Nell saw a remarkable difference in rapport with her staff. "If you had told me that one nonverbal behavior could make that much difference, I wouldn't have believed you," she said. "Now I do!"

Women at my seminar often ask what they can do if they've clearly given a negative first impression. I advise them to make a clean break with their old behavior and image. Take a few days of vacation, come back with a new haircut, a new style of dressing, even new glasses — anything that will help others "see" you again instead of judging you through their old mental images.

For a few days, go out of your way to project new behavior as well as your new visual image. The purpose of this chapter is to examine both verbal and nonverbal communication: how we use things like our body posture, facial expression, eye contact or touch, as well as our speech, to communicate with others. There are two messages we send nonverbally: the ones we intentionally send, and those we don't realize we're sending. If the impression people have of us is positive, if we communicate confidence, authority and positive power, then that first impression continues to gather benefits. But a negative impression is difficult — and sometimes impossible — to change.

Begin to learn how you communicate nonverbally. While you can't control things like your skin color, gender or age, you can deal with the way you use your physical appearance, the personal space around you, touch, eye contact and facial expressions. These nonverbals often give an impression stronger than your words. The latest research in this area shows that 55 percent of communication is made up of facial expressions and body language alone. Thirty-eight percent of your message is communicated by the volume, pitch, rate, word choice and articulation of your speech. The actual word content of your message accounts for only seven percent of the communication! If people do not like what they see in your appearance or hear in your voice, they may not stay around to listen to your ideas.

Nonverbals can communicate power, authority and confidence, and allow people to focus on the content of your message instead of wondering, "Does she have the authority or knowledge to say that?"

Nonverbals can also strongly affect first impressions. People form opinions of others in the first 30-40 seconds of meeting them, and those opinions tend to be so firm as to prejudice any subsequent information received.

Professional interviewers may interview 400 to 500 people, from whom they select only four or five. The interviewers may make the decision not to hire in the first 30 seconds of meeting the applicant. The decision to hire takes a lot longer, but the decision to reject can be made that quickly.

You have probably done much the same thing. At a social gathering, have you ever said to yourself, "I don't know who is interesting here, but I can tell it's definitely not the one in the white socks, or that one, or that one..."?

Information about you is transmitted nonverbally in only 30 seconds. You can't talk fast enough to pull yourself out of a negative first impression. So it's best to make your appearance work for you. Consider the way you carry yourself, the way you move. What do you do with the space around you? Powerful, confident people use an open body posture, they spread out and take up space. (Did you ever sit next to someone on an airplane who took both armrests?) Yet women are taught to constrict their bearing and take up as little space as possible — crossed legs, one tightly hugging the other, both pulled in close to the chair. Women broadcast the nonverbal message, "I'm just taking up a tiny little corner. Is it okay if I stay?"

To convey confidence, use an asymmetrical open body posture. Seated, it means legs parallel and feet flat on the floor, arms open and asymmetrical, e.g., one on the desk and one on the arm of the chair. Standing, it means legs slightly apart, about even with your armpits. Bend your elbows and keep your hands in your pockets (notice how that opens up your body posture) or bend your arms and hold them loosely in front of you. This may feel awkward at first, but it looks confident and well-grounded. A mental image to keep is that of a general in the military. Imagine a general trying to command while standing like many women do, toes pointed slightly out, one foot behind the other, arms at his side. Take mental snapshots of yourself several times day. What nonverbal message would a stranger receive from your bearing?

Eye contact is probably the most extensively researched area in nonverbal communication. However, it is an area where the information is complex and sometimes contradictory. Direct, level eye contact is an important indicator of confidence. We call people who don't easily meet our gaze "shy" or "shifty." At the least, we say they lack confidence; at the worst, that they are lying. Yet women are told not to stare, and that looking directly into a man's eyes implies availability. Because a direct gaze is a power symbol, women often modify and soften it by quickly lowering their eyes, looking to the side, or tilting their heads. A direct, confident, level gaze, held about 50 percent of the time, is a power gesture women need to use more often.

Research shows that women look at men more than men look at women, but the gaze of a woman is often one of subordinate attentiveness and approval seeking. We watch men to look for cues from the powerful. Does he like what I'm saying? Am I coming on too strong? Remember also that gaze aversion, what etiquette books would call "ladylike behavior," is also subordinate behavior. According to one study, when men and women passed each other, 71 percent of the men established eye contact with the women, but only 43 percent of the women did so with the men. See if you can up those odds. If eye contact is difficult for you, try looking anywhere in the upper third of a person's face. This usually is perceived as eye contact. Too much direct eye contact, however, may present you as being too critical or demanding of others, for people feel put on the spot or examined when eye contact is too intense.

Another important nonverbal communicator is your facial expression. Your thoughts are expressed on your face unless you make a conscious effort to hide or disguise them with a false or contrived expression. The expressionless face draws no attention and communicates nothing, and a blank expression suggests an equally blank thought.

The most used and misused facial expression is the smile. Our smiles lose their power when we use them too often, but an honestly happy expression invites association. However, a smile is not always a sign of happiness or pleasure. It can imply that the person smiling feels in some way subordinate to the other. In one study, young children responded to the question, "Why do men smile?" with, "Because they are happy." When asked why women smile, they said, "Women smile all the time."

Begin monitoring your smiles. If you find they are not the result of happiness, contentment or expectancy of progress, but are an attempt to appease others, stop them.

If I were to ask you why we touch one another, you would probably say to show friendship, affection, support, perhaps even sexuality. To show power and dominance might not be two words you would choose. But let's examine touch more closely. Would you be more likely to walk over to the boss and put a hand on her shoulder while discussing a project, or would the boss be more likely to do so to you? Far from just showing affection and support, touch is also a primary way by which dominance is reinforced. Let me stress that power can be reinforced through touch without an obvious intention to do so. The boss may be feeling genuinely affectionate and supportive when she puts her hand on your shoulder, but as long as the touch is nonreciprocal, dominance is also reinforced. Nonreciprocal touch shows one-sided power in a relationship, and is something first to be aware of, then modified or corrected. Reciprocal touch, however, is a wholesome form of nonverbal communication. In one study on touch, men and women were given silhouettes of their bodies and were told, "Take these around with you over the next couple of weeks and every time strangers touch you, color in where they do so." Guess who came back colored in black and blue! Keep tabs on how many times you are touched and are not reciprocating, and how often touch is used to reinforce power relationships around you.

Another study that related touch closely to the business setting was done at a library. In this study they asked the librarian to touch every other person who checked out a book. Now, a librarian couldn't do much, probably just graze your hand or brush your sleeve as she was passing your library card in the book back to you. They coded those library cards and monitored the return rate on them. What do you think happened? There was a significant difference in return rate by just that much touch. The people who were touched brought their books back to the library more promptly. Furthermore, one researcher standing outside the library posed as a funding source person from the city council. He asked those leaving the library what they thought of that library. The people that had not been touched said, "It's a library." But the people who had been touched said, "You know, now that I think of it, this is a very helpful library. The people here are always friendly." A small amount of touch produced a significant difference in response.

Consider the handshake, one of the most commonly accepted forms of touching. The confident handshake is firm, warm and predictable. There's nothing halfway about it. That means the fold of skin where the thumb joins the hand meets the other person's. Since many men (and some women) are still uncertain about shaking hands with women, we have to stride forward with our right arm clearly extended to signal our intent. Follow the rules of business, not social etiquette. Stand up when you shake hands in a business setting, do not remain seated like a "lady." For the next couple of days, shake hands with as many different people as possible and note how you respond to limp, "cold fish" handshakes. Note, too, the immediate impression you make.

When you mirror others, instead of simply showing the other person how to be, you begin to synchronize your movements and mirror the other person. Eventually, in rapport, you reflect each other. This deeper level of mirroring I liken to the synchronization stage of Timothy Perper's research. Perper was a biologist working on his PhD. He must have thought that things were getting boring in the biology lab and that he needed to perk things up some because he said: "You know how birds have a mating dance? How birds have a series of steps they have to do in a certain order or else they all go home to separate bedrooms? Let's look and see if there is a human mating dance." Calling on all of his communicative powers, Perper convinced his dissertation committee of the need for this research and he headed off to a random sampling of single bars where he observed 500 couples from the time they were clearly strangers to the time they were clearly a couple in rapport. Now if you went out to a singles bar tonight, purely for research purposes, and you looked at twosomes all lined across the bar, you could probably say, "Those two people just happen to have chairs next to each other, but those two people are a couple." You could pick them out. Something special defines a couple.

Perper says there are four stages that people go through before rapport is established between them, before they become "a couple." The first stage is obviously the approach. Someone has to approach the other one. The second stage Perper calls the swivel. He observed that a couple is not a couple as long as one or both of them are facing the bartender. They are not performing the swivel until both turn and are in direct alignment with each other — not obliquely aligned, not almost aligned, but in direct alignment with each other. That sounds simple enough, but if you monitor yourself over the next couple of days you will probably find that you seldom are in direct alignment with another person while seated adjacently in conversation. Once alignment has been achieved, the physical barrier between two people must be broken. Stage three is the touch. The touch can be as simple an act as brushing the other person's sleeve or just grazing their hand, but physical contact must occur before stage four, synchronization, can be accomplished. It is evident when Perper's synchronization, what I also call mirroring, is taking place between two people. They might both pick up their glasses and drink at the same time, take off their jackets and put them on the back of their chairs simultaneously, both rest their head in their hands or cross and recross their legs together. When each begins to synchronize and mirror the behavior of the other, the couple is "in sync" and rapport is established. Reflection of one another becomes natural, behavior becomes concordant, and the couple is "a couple." The question concerning rapport is: Do you have to wait for things to happen, or can you take control and bring stages 1, 2, 3 and

4 into your experience? Can you approach? Can you swivel? Can you touch? Can you synchronize?

Most of us can handle the first three steps, but the final synchronization stage is more difficult than may be realized. Try a quick experiment: Cross your arms comfortably in front of your chest. Now cross them in the other direction. If changing your own behavior just slightly was harder than you anticipated, you can see that changing your behavior to mirror that of another can be even more of a test. However, there are a number of things about a person you can mirror. Mirror something about a person that stays fairly stationary, such as a facial expression, the way they hold their body, the way they sit, or the way they rest their head. Or, you can be more subtle and mirror someone's speech pattern. Generally, less attention is paid to one's speech than to one's body, and you are less likely to be noticed in your mirroring efforts. Mirroring of speech patterns is considered a sophisticated level of synchronization. The rate, volume, enthusiasm level, jargon or intonation variances of speech all can be mirrored.

Now that you're clear on what mirroring or synchronization is, let's examine how it can be effective in terms of communication: You have come home from work at the end of "one of those days," and all you really want to do is just sit on the couch and gripe for a little while. You just want to tell someone, "Would you please listen to what a hero I have been for having lived through this day? Just listen to me for a while." Enter your companion, for whom it has been a great, stupendous, successful day! You let out about two sentences of tension when Mr. Joyous says, "Oh, come on. It can't have been that bad. Cheer up!" If you immediately say, "You're right. I don't feel depressed after all. I'm just fine!" you have been successfully drawn out of your low position by "pacing." You have caught the enthusiasm level of your companion. Sometimes contagion works, but with two such disparate moods as in this scene, pacing probably is not going to work. You still want to be heard in the midst of your despair. If, however, your companion drops down to your level and demonstrates rapport with you for a few minutes, if you are shown compassion for just a short while, would you keep on griping? You would probably soon say,

"Oh, come on. Let's cheer up and go fix some dinner." You see, mirroring is a useful skill. The successful practice of synchronization can break the bonds of negativity and open the door to more positive feelings and actions.

Crisis center volunteers are trained to meet their phone callers at the caller's level of enthusiasm. Those in crisis are genuinely depressed and respond poorly to the volunteer who replies to a call for help with, "Oh, come on. Cheer up. Things can't be that bad." Some semblance of rapport must first be established. Dropping to the caller's level of enthusiasm enables the volunteer to be in sync with the caller and the caller is more likely to follow the next thought process the volunteer models.

When you feel out of sync with another person, try using their level of enthusiasm, mood or manner as your own. As you synchronize and mirror their behavior you will either be drawn up to their level of thought and action, or you will establish a trust level where you can begin to draw them to a higher level.

Besides mirroring physical aspects or speech patterns, you can mirror thought processes. Not what they think, but how they think. There is an interesting branch of psychology called neuro-linguistic programming which deals with how people process information, or think. NLP's founders, Richard Banlor and John Grinder, say that everyone has a different system for receiving, storing and retrieving information. If you were aware of how people operated, you could feed information into their systems properly, much the same as you program information into a computer, and communication would be correctly channeled at the outset. If I knew which system you ran on, I would give you information your system would understand, not mine.

Some of you reading this chapter are visually-oriented people. You walk around with cameras in your heads and you snap pictures of everything that goes on around you. Then you file all those pictures and when asked to remember something, you pull out a photograph and look at it. If you have to imagine something, you make a new photograph. Others of you are auditory people. You have tape recorders going in your mind all the time and you record everything around you. When asked to remember something, you pull out a tape and listen to it. And others of you are kinesthetic people. You process information by touching or feeling everything and filing it that way. When asked to remember something, you bring to mind how it felt — not the emotion, but the touch of it. NLP teaches you to follow how people think by watching their eye movements, but let me share an easier way with you. While not foolproof, it usually works. You simply have to listen to people, because they walk around broadcasting their style all the time, although few pay attention. Do you, in fact, know what your style is? You probably broadcast it every day as well.

Visually-oriented people use visual phrases like "That *looks* good to me," "I need to get the *big picture* on that," "from my *point of view*," "it was as *clear* as day," "I *saw* the light at the end of the tunnel," "the *light* suddenly came on." You will hear auditory people saying things like: "That *sounds* good to me," "do you *hear* what I'm saying?" (as opposed to "Do you see what I mean?"), "that *rings* true," "you can *say* that again," "we're not in *tune* on this project," "there's no *harmony* around this office." Kinesthetic people, feeling people, broadcast their style by saying: "That just *feels* right," "I can't get a good *handle* on that," "I can't *grasp* what you're saying," "that's a *sharp* idea," "that's *fuzzy* thinking," "*run* that by me again." Can you feel how those are all kinesthetic terms? Most people have one prevalent mode of processing information and about 70 percent of the time they will put given information into their own terms and process it in their own style. However, we each use all three styles along the way. For instance, if you were asked what color your mother's eyes were, you would call on a visual piece of information for your answer, but if the query were: "What was your mother like when you were growing up?" you would respond in accordance with your particular style of retrieving information. You would primarily recall what she looked like, how she sounded or what it felt like being near her. Each of us accesses information in our own way when given the chance. It's important to be aware of this and to know how other people process their information — how they think. A great many misunderstandings can come about if you do not.

Consider what visual people need to see to know that you are really listening to them, to know that you respect what they are saying. The visual person wants eye contact. On the other hand, auditory people frequently turn their ear slightly toward the other person when totally involved in listening to the information being given. And if you are really there for those of the kinesthetic family, if you are listening to them and care about what they're saying, you reach out and touch their hand or pat them on the shoulder. The kinesthetic person wants touch. You may be broadcasting your style clearly to another person, and that person may have no idea that the signal is being given. An example: A couple comes in for marriage counseling. She's visual and he's kinesthetic. She begins with: "I get no respect around the household — I mean, nobody sees anything that I do! It's like I'm invisible, and I can't see staying in this marriage!" Her husband tries to reassure her that he really does care, and he reaches over and touches her. The woman turns to him and says, "I didn't ask you to paw me in public! What I asked was for you to see what I contribute around the house!" Husband and wife are both operating out of their own systems, but neither is aware of the other's style. To the woman, respect and attention are eye contact. To the man, interest and caring are touch. She's visual. He's kinesthetic.

Here is another example: Your boss may be a visual person. If you go to her and simply talk about what you're thinking, you may not reach her. If, on the other hand, you put something in writing and let her look at it first, so she can clearly see what you propose, she will probably say, "Talk to me more about this. What do you see going on here? What's the idea behind it?"

Learn the styles of those with whom you work. It's especially helpful to know how others think when you are dealing with negative or difficult information. If the information is negative, you have just the information hurdle to overcome. Why have two systems going against you? At least be able to communicate in the other person's style. Be certain you know what your style is, too. Then broadcast it clearly. Here are a couple of ways that may help you determine what your main method of processing information is:

When you're given directions to a nearby restaurant, do you say, "Let me see a map. Until I can see it on a map, I have no idea where I'm going." Or do you respond, "Don't show me those little squiggly blue lines, just tell me. Do I walk out of here to the stop light and turn right or left?" Or are you the kinesthetic person who replies, "Wait a minute. Until I can get a pencil and write it down for myself (until I can move my body around the information), I'm not going to remember a word."

Here's a second way to help you determine how you process information. How do you remember a telephone number without actually writing it down? Do you see the numbers run across your mind? Do you hear the number and record it in your memory? Or, is it necessary for you to trace the numbers on your knee or perhaps punch the buttons on the telephone in your mind? It's a very sophisticated level of synchronization to be able to mirror the way in which another person thinks and it is extremely effective if you can use it. It's one of the secrets of exceptional counselors and therapists and one way they build almost legendary rapport with their clients. Polish up your looking glass and see if you can establish rapport with others more quickly and easily.

Step #5
Dealing With Conflict Confidently

by Connie Merritt

S omewhere along the way to reaching your career dreams, you're going to "butt heads" with difficult people: bosses whose favorite form of communication is screaming; customers who are never satisfied; subordinates who agree with everything, yet do nothing; coworkers who rip you to shreds behind your back.

Sounds like fun, right? For what it's worth, we all have difficult people in our lives. This chapter isn't a top secret Master Plan to have all the difficult people shipped to Mars. But it is a good blueprint of the types of people who create conflict, why they act the way they do, and how you can confidently deal with them.

People have been trying to figure out people for a long time (why did Eve give Adam that *apple*? Why not a banana?). Astrology was really big in the old days. It grouped people into "signs" based on how the stars were aligned at the time of their birth. Even today, many people subscribe to astrology, and let's face it, it's fun to peek at our horoscopes in the morning newspaper.

Hippocrates believed that people were the way they were because of the proportion of fluids in their bodies. He described people as being one of four temperaments: sanguine (the "cheerful" type because of lots of healthy blood in their bodies); melancholic (the "gloomy" sort — who wouldn't be with all that black bile?); phlegmatic (a bit sluggish); and choleric (the type that's quick-tempered — I guess they didn't like being called choleric).

It's not really practical today for you to check out a person's level of black bile or chart his or her star sign in order to deal with conflict confidently. Fortunately, there's a much better way.

Our behavior is based on our needs. It makes sense, then, that the more adept you become at meeting the needs of others (and, of course, yourself), the better you'll be at handling difficult people.

Everyone has his or her own way of doing things. We act the way we think. Our actions take on a pattern because we behave in a similar style over and over. I'll prove it. Right now, lay the book aside and clasp your hands in front of you. Which thumb is on top? Okay, now unclasp them and try it again with the other thumb on top. Feels awkward, doesn't it? Nevertheless, the result is the same: your hands are clasped. So even though we fall into patterns of doing things or reacting in certain ways, we can learn different responses.

How do you react when you're confronted by conflict? Do you feel helpless or do you feel like fuming? When the boss blows up at you for the 531st time, do you bolster yourself for the 532nd or do you wonder if there might be an easier way to deal with him or her?

There is an easier way. It's called coping. And when you learn how to do it (after reading this chapter), you're going to stand up to difficult people on *equal* terms. You're not going to change them, but you will take away some of their power.

Let's look now at four common behavior types, how they can make our lives miserable and what we can do about them.

Those Hard-Headed Drivers

Keith, your manager, is a real thorn in your side. He changes direction in the middle of a project and becomes aggressive and demanding under the slightest pressure. If he's not always in the limelight, he sulks. Besides being a thorn in your side, Keith is, in your view, a major barrier to your advancement.

Drivers are ulcer-giving, headache-inducing, dictatorial bullies. None of us chooses to subject ourselves to their tantrums, insults, criticism and unreasonable demands. But what if you work with one? Or live with one? Fear not. Here are some ideas on how to deal with them.

Drivers are easy to pick out, even in a crowd. They'll be talking more than anyone else in the room and making blunt statements. They use their clothes and jewelry as "status symbols." They seem to fill a room because they look as though they're taking up a lot of space.

When Drivers aren't being difficult, their behavior still leans toward restlessness, quick reactions, outspokenness and aggressiveness. Their workspace is formal, efficient and highly structured. They operate at a fast, decisive pace and go after measurable results as a high priority. Their motto could be: "If you don't blow your own horn, someone will use it as a spittoon."

Drivers' biggest fear is a loss of control. Knowing that, do everything you can to avoid making them feel as if they don't hold the reins. They love success, winning and power — their three prime motivators.

People can change but don't expect them to just because that's what *you* want. That being the case, modify your own behavior since you know what this type of person needs. When working with a Driver, remember to:

1. Get right to the point.
2. Do your homework. Give them the facts, figures and specifics.
3. Deliver the material in a no-nonsense style, keeping the pace fast.
4. Be able to answer questions about time, schedule and costs.

5. Ask direct, purposeful questions.
6. Establish guidelines for quality, give bottom-line desired results and then get out of the way. Drivers hate people hovering over them.
7. Keep them informed of tangible progress.

Dealing with Conflict with Drivers

Despite your best working form, Drivers will still blow up at times. But you can stand up to them. Here are a few pointers:

1. *Let them go ahead and throw a tantrum.* Wait them out, looking directly at them. They might feel embarrassed after they run out of steam. Your silence can be powerful. If you're really brave, ask, "Anything else?"

2. *Invite them to sit down.* Asking them to sit down is a way of disarming them without making them feel like they've lost control. If they remain standing, make sure you're eye to eye. Try not to posture yourself defensively, that is, no crossed arms, hands on hips, frown or squinted eyes.

3. *If they interrupt, hang in there by saying, "You interrupted me!" repeatedly if necessary.* Ever been in a conversation where the Driver insists on interrupting or even carries on a side conversation during your presentation? Use this technique, but use it carefully. The really heavy Drivers construe it as usurping their control.

4. *Call their name to gain their attention.* One of the most powerful words you can say to anyone is his or her name. If a Driver is attacking you or interrupting repeatedly or throwing a tantrum, a loud and clear, "John!" might be just the thing for snapping him out of it.

5. *If they're trying to intimidate you, visualize them standing there in the wildest underwear you can imagine.* Crazy as this sounds, it works. Who could be intimidated by a grown man standing in front of you in a pair of purple polka-dotted boxer shorts?

6. *If they attack you indirectly, ask them if they meant what they said.* Another way Drivers exercise control is with biting sarcasm and snide remarks. They think they're being clever. So ask him, in your best naivete, "That wasn't meant as a dig, was it, George?"

7. *When they attack you directly in front of a group, ask the group if they agree.* "Does anyone else see it that way?" If no one does, you've taken the sting out of the attack. If the group *does* agree, at least you've opened it up to discussion and still diluted the attack.

8. *Give them alternative chances for success.* Drivers love to win and look good to other people. If they can't see "success" at the end of a task, they withdraw. So give them alternative action plans and let *them* choose.

9. *Argue with facts, not feelings.* Presenting facts keeps the conversation on a non-personal level. This is just fine with Drivers since they like to give the impression that feelings don't have a place in their world. Actually, a gruff exterior often covers up a vulnerable, insecure person with *lots* of hidden feelings. If you try to bring feelings into the picture, though, you threaten their control of the situation. So keep cool and "Just the facts, Ma'am."

10. *State precisely what you've agreed upon.* Make sure you're clear about what is wanted and what is expected. "Okay, Marge, as I understand it, you'll do the sales reports for the Midwest region by next Wednesday and I'll take it from there and write a summary report due four days later. Is that how you see it? Did I leave out anything?" Just to be sure, put it all down in a memo.

Remember that the Driver's greatest fear is loss of control. When you spot a Driver, anticipate conflict ahead. Plan your action and keep these tips in mind.

Non-Producing "Yes" People and Other Sociables

If you think Drivers are good at creating conflict, here's a completely different type: Sociables. They're the people you can't help liking, yet your stress level skyrockets when you're around them. Do they sound familiar?

Susan, one of your top salespeople, is a charmer — outgoing, pleasant — the customers love her. But to get her to finish month-end reports on time or plan her sales prospects is like pulling teeth. When the tension level is high, she gets even more disorganized and emotional.

If anyone could be described as the "life of the party," it's your husband. Everyone loves good ol', affable Hank. He always has time for making sure everybody else is enjoying themselves. But every time you try to plan buying your first home together, he just gets sarcastic.

Maddening, aren't they?

Across the room you see the Sociables. They smile often and "talk" with their hands. They're the "huggy," "touchy" type. They seem to carry a portable party around with them. Lots of one-liner jokes fall out of their mouths, at times quite caustic. They'll do just about anything to grab someone's attention. Their motto could be: "Notice me."

Look around their offices or homes and you'll see clutter, yet they're warm and welcoming. You'll notice memorabilia or personal accolades on the walls.

Since we're calling them Sociables, their need to be around people is obvious. A surefire way to get them to "bloom" is by offering praise, recognition or outright applause!

A Sociable's greatest fear is loss of social status. They'll do anything to avoid losing your approval. When they're under a great deal of stress and they try too hard, they come across as superficial, over-eager and "flighty" in their thoughts. All they want to do is hear more "applause."

You'll run across Sociables every day. Here are six tips for dealing with this type in general, non-conflict situations:

1. When they do something right, "overload" them with credit and praise.

2. Make them feel like they're part of what's happening. Share important information with them.

3. When they feel like talking (which is often), let them. It's one of the things they do best.

4. They love physical signs of approval. Shake their hand, pat them on the back, touch their arm. They'll respond favorably.

5. Incentive gifts and prizes work wonders with Sociables. They like to be paid well, too (but who doesn't?).

6. Share your personal feelings. Sociables like to be friends.

Dealing with Conflict with Sociables

Try to imagine getting into conflict with John Denver or Goldie Hawn. They're fun, nice, wonderful people — but that doesn't mean they won't do things that could drive you up the wall. When they do, here are some options for you:

1. *If they're habitually late, help them set realistic time frames for getting tasks done.* Life's a party for Sociables and who cares what time it is when there's a party going on? That means you're the one who has to offer some time structure. If you expect them for an important appointment, try saying, "You know, I've never been able to make it from the airport in less than an hour. Should we say four o'clock?" Or be sneaky: Tell them the appointment's a half hour before you really expect them.

2. *Make honesty easy for them.* Sociables tend to "stretch the truth" and exaggerate sometimes. It's not really lying as far as they're concerned — it's just making the story more interesting so people will like them. When this happens, try to open the door for honesty: "Margaret over in Accounting had a problem almost like yours. She tried this. Does that sound like it would work for you?"

3. *When they're sarcastic, cool off and confront them later in private.* "Oh, the slings and arrows of outrageous sarcasm!" (My apologies to W. Shakespeare.) Sarcasm can hurt. When Sociables start using it, look for the hidden message. Give yourself a chance to calm down, but go back to them later and deal with the message. "Joan, you are the greatest to have around here. I really appreciate your spontaneity and enthusiasm. In one way or another, I've been accused of being too stuffy. Do you have any ideas how I could loosen up?" Ask your question, then shut up. Sociables love to talk, so you'll get a lot of information.

4. *When their plans take on grandiose, unrealistic proportions, give them an "out."* Don't let a Sociable's charm and convincing manner lead you or your company down the primrose path. Bring in an "expert" — whether it's an article, solid proof or a consultant in that particular area.

5. *When they're in a stalling or time-wasting mood, ask direct questions.* Stalling's a sign that something else is wrong. The only

way to find out is by asking them. "What's going on here, Sue?" "How do you feel about that change, Marian?" Make it as easy as possible for them to tell you. Be forewarned: Despite your best efforts, Sociables will rarely tell you what's really wrong.

6. *If their course of action is wasting your time, show them how a re-direction can earn them praise.* This is really dangling the carrot at the end of the stick, but it works on Sociables. "Janie, last year when we faced this challenge, Jeff made just three more calls daily and won the sales contest." Sociables will go for the prize and acclaim.

7. *If they make an impulsive decision, give them more time.* Sociables prefer getting on with the "party of life" over making difficult decisions. Rather than force them to act impulsively, say something like, "This is a tough decision, isn't it? If I were in your shoes, I'd feel exactly the same. Why don't we take the weekend to mull it over and settle it next Monday?"

8. *If they take "pot shots" at you in a public situation, tell them what they did — non-threateningly.* Sociables are insecure people. Their insecurity sometimes forces them to lash out at the people who are really important to them. When this happens, take a deep breath, lighten your voice, smile and say, "I can't believe how you come up with those funny lines. It couldn't be that I'm really a nerd, could it?"

9. *If their behavior is continually difficult, try this: make them your friend.* One of the best tips I received from my grandmother was how to get people to talk about themselves. She said (and I've found it to be true) when you get them talking you might find out something you have in common. Grabbing a small thread might be all it takes to break the ice. Ask them: "If you could put your finger on three things to which you can attribute your success (positive attitude/happiness/curly hair), what would those be?"

10. *When they get emotional, let them get it all out.* When a Sociable's heart is in overload, the best thing you can do is listen while they talk. Keep on listening. A hug works wonders, too.

Those Agreeable Team Players

Boy, did you get a deal when you married your husband! He's reliable, always honest — the "Marcus Welby" of husbands. He's always agreeable. That's the problem. You say you want to vacation at the beach this year instead of the mountains. He says "fine," but you can never pin him down on dates and plans. Finally, his agreeable stalling has made it too late to make any trip reservations. Maybe that's what he wanted all the time.

For six months you have been working with Betsy to find the perfect home. You pride yourself on how much your clients like you. For several afternoons you've scoured the town together and become friends in the process. You know exactly what Betsy wants and it finally comes onto the market. You try to reach her for hours, then the house is sold from under your nose. Through the real estate grapevine you find out Betsy bought it from another agent. You're flabbergasted. She doesn't return your calls. When you finally reach her, she says her neighbor, new to the business, needed the encouragement of a sale. But, of course, she appreciates all your work and will definitely buy her next house through you. Betsy tries to please everyone — but you're the one without a commission.

Conflict with Team Players doesn't involve back-stabbing or nasty remarks or temper tantrums. You hardly know you're in conflict until you recognize their inability to make a decision and their "wishy-washy" behavior.

What do Team Players want? To feel valued in a relationship. When they're forced to do something they think will affect the quality of a relationship, *that's* when they become difficult. They absolutely hate confrontation: "Oh, please don't confront me because that means we're all not getting along and that means I might lose my security." They center their world around the security of home, job and family. Their definition of success is having deep personal relationships and getting along with everyone around them.

It's hard to imagine the Team Player having a "hot button." Even when they're under a lot of stress, they're still sooo darn nice! Conflict can arise, though, so here's what you can do to avoid it:

1. Keep your pace slow; make them feel comfortable and secure with you.

2. Avoid using words or actions that threaten your interpersonal relationship.
3. Give them loads of personal assurance and support.
4. Sprinkle the conversation with ''how'' questions.
5. They want to be possessive of their job, family or project. So let them.
6. Be patient and sensitive toward them.
7. Don't rock the boat; they're content with the status quo.

Dealing with Conflict with Team Players

All the Team Player really wants is for everybody to get along. When their fear of losing this keeps them from making a decision or has them leaning one way then the other, you've got yourself a conflict.

How do you train a puppy dog? When it makes a mistake, you scold it. Then it turns around and looks up at you with those sweet, sorrowful eyes. But you stand your ground, right? You're tough. Just when you think you've got it licked, the little darling does something so loving and cute, what can you do but give in? In case you haven't noticed, there are lots of adult dogs in the world. They made it past puppyhood because they're so cute. That's what you're dealing with in Team Players. So when conflict arises, here's what you can do:

1. *If they stall, give them instructions and lead them in the right direction.* They'll do anything to please you because your relationship means so much to them. So say something like, ''This is such a pleasure working with you like this. I wouldn't want anything to change that, so can we work on this project two hours each day until we get it all done? I'm sure the two of us can meet the deadline.''

2. *When they pull their ''wishy-washy'' act, let them know you're there to help.* Team Players' indecisiveness eats up valuable time and lets a problem get blown out of proportion. But it's really hard for them to ask for help because they don't want to look stupid or risk rejection. Try saying, ''Ann, I don't know if I could do that all alone like you're doing. Please feel free to ask me for help. I'd

be happy to work on it with you.''

3. *When they acquiesce, give them choices.* When you realize someone is going along with everything you say, force them (gently) into making a choice. ''You know, Paul, I'm not too crazy about this convention spot. What do you think about Oshkosh or Nome? Let me know because your input is really important to the company.''

4. *If you want them to take on more responsibilities but can't offer more money, give them perks.* To Team Players, a perk shows them they belong or are loved. They like feeling they're important in the grand scheme of things. So give them their own parking spaces, name plates — things that symbolize ''We're glad you're here.''

5. *When they're being non-responsive, take them out of the situation and do something purely social.* Prodding a Team Player by asking ''why, why, why'' just won't work. You'll have a better chance of breaking through their non-responsive shield by doing something as simple as going for a walk or shopping with them. Make them feel accepted and there's a good chance they'll open up.

6. *When they pout, pay them a compliment that means something to them.* It's not just children who pout; adults do, too, especially the Team Players. Pouting occurs when they're feeling a lack of love or acceptance. Even though you'd like to throw them across your knee and give them a good paddling, restrain yourself. Instead, say something like, ''You're such a good friend. I want us to get along always. What's going on now?''

7. *If someone is being rude or insensitive to them, intervene as a third party.* Team Players love harmony so they rarely fight back. But watch out: Later you might have to bear their withdrawal or hesitancy. To keep that from happening, jump into the situation with something like, ''Didn't we have to be back at the office by noon, Rob?'' Later explain it just wasn't worth staying around that rude person.

8. *Use ''buzzwords'' that are ''music to their ears.''* We all like the sound of certain words and Team Players are no exception. Here are a few that really work on them: definite, positive, certain, optimistic, needed, necessary, growing and permanent.

Perfectionists and Nit-Pickers

Every office seems to have a resident grouch like Gloria. She wants explanations to every statement, goes strictly by the book and never cracks a smile. A hard worker, Gloria is always taking care of business. Expect the freeze from her if you have to correct or question her work. It's nice to have her attend to the details, but you find little that is warm and personable about her. Sort of like working with Mr. Spock from *Star Trek*.

What a hectic day! You've spent hours preparing for dinner guests. It's been hard work, but you're pleased with the results and look forward to a pleasant evening. Then your husband walks in and casually mentions that the spices aren't "quite right" in the pesto sauce and the Levelor blinds are dusty and a few other "little things." You pick up on his negativity and try to discuss it with him. But he immediately "clams up" and the conversation comes to a screeching halt.

Perfectionists can be even more frustrating and difficult than Drivers. At least Drivers let you know what's happening. Perfectionists earn the nickname "The Turtle" because they tend to figuratively crawl into their shells, making any solution to the conflict hard to find.

How do you spot a Perfectionist? In a roomful of people, they're the ones not smiling. They're quiet, nonverbal, definitely non-"touchy" and expressionless. They move with such caution you're tempted to put a mirror under their nose to see if it fogs. They appear fragile, unconfident, walking with stooped shoulders and their heads looking downward.

The world needs Perfectionists because they're such hard workers. They're detail-oriented, task-driven, precise, analytical and well-organized. They're the type with every favorite recipe neatly and alphabetically cataloged and cross-referenced.

Is it any wonder that a Perfectionist's greatest joy in life comes from being correct? Or that his biggest fear is being embarrassed? Perfectionists take pride in their competence, so if you imply otherwise, they can't handle it. They see their thoroughness and loyalty as the way to gain acceptance.

Perfectionists don't give any clues to the outside world because they don't want their thoughts invaded. Surprisingly, though, they're quite intuitive. Maybe it's from collecting all that data (they love data) so they have more information to put into an "educated guess."

Perfectionists are going to be your challenge. More than any of the other types we've discussed, Perfectionists need handling with "kid gloves." Remember a few basic rules:

1. Deal with them on a one-to-one basis, if at all possible.
2. Speak more formally than you usually do and keep your personal opinions to yourself.
3. Control your animated expressions and avoid touching them (sounds horribly unfriendly; I don't mean it to be).
4. Be patient, patient and more patient!
5. Give them logical explanations.
6. Stick to the business at hand and assure them they're "right."

Dealing with Conflict with Perfectionists

Perfectionists like surprises about as much as Dracula likes daylight. When surprise or unpredictability enters their lives, they can become difficult to deal with. Consider:

1. *When their thoroughness causes them to miss deadlines, guide them toward timeliness.* Perfectionists don't immediately see timeliness as being applicable to them. Accuracy is what's of prime importance to them. What you need to do is let them know how important their expertise is to the task and that the deadline is critical. Ask them how you can help them meet it.

2. *If they become resentful and hold a grudge, just let go.* Usually a grudge is held against someone who's criticized their work, especially if it was done in front of other people. To the Perfectionist, this is the "unpardonable sin." Sorry, but you'll rarely win them back. The best you can do is forget it and go on.

3. *If they "lash out" at you, back down.* This is a rare occurrence since emotion and animation aren't parts of their personality. When it does happen, they're feeling like a cornered animal. Maybe

they think a deadline's too tight for them to do a job the way they think it should be done. Don't jump into the ring ready for a boxing match. Instead, give them space and ask, "How much time do you need to do this job well?"

4. *When they start whining, pick out the valid complaints.* It's not easy listening to a constant complainer. Use your best listening skills to hear what's worth their complaining and then try to offer solutions.

5. *When they withdraw, ask open-ended questions.* "Yes" and "no" questions only give them the chance to further withdraw or evade the issue. Ask "how," "what" and "why" questions and then silently wait for their answer. Don't let them off the hook. The silence will be tougher on them than on you.

6. *Meet their skepticism with details and explanations.* Perfectionists don't see how anyone could possibly do a job as well as they can. So give them what they want: lots of documentation and details (they secretly want to put their families on flow charts).

7. *Confront them when they start throwing blame and excuses.* Perfectionists want others to think they're perfect, yet they're filled with self-doubt. Deal with them in private, asking, "Do you think there isn't enough time to do this project?" or "How do you think Jim's mistake can be rectified?" If you're the one being blamed, try, "The pressure of this responsibility is really making my job more difficult. Please tell me how I can make my job run more smoothly."

8. *When they're negative, they're not ready to act.* Don't impose tight deadlines and sketchy background on them. Remember how they love thoroughness and accuracy. Simply ask, "How do you think we can handle this situation?"

9. *Avoid words that strike terror in their heart.* Stay away from words that connote lack of harmony, such as: "laid off," "not needed," "useless," "uncertain," "leaving."

The Goodbye Alternative

You're probably thinking now, "Well, I can march into the office tomorrow and handle Bill — he's definitely the Driver type.

And just wait 'til I see Barbara at the next board meeting; she's such a nit-picker.''

Now that you recognize certain types of behavior, you can handle conflict more confidently. But let's talk about one more alternative.

Even more important than knowing the type of person who's creating the conflict is knowing your own limits. Just how much can you really accomplish in the situation? Trust your judgment. Take a good look around. Sometimes the very best, smartest thing you can do is turn around and walk away. Don't think for a minute that's "chickening out." On the contrary, it's making the world work for you with careful positioning, timing and strategy.

When are the times to consider the "Goodbye Alternative?" If you find yourself in a situation in which you feel you don't belong, walk away as soon as you realize it makes no sense for you to be there. Don't waste time trying to convince yourself "they'll come around to my way of thinking."

Another situation worth walking away from is when it's clear that someone refuses to listen to you. Why in the world should you put yourself through such degradation? Give yourself more credit and head straight for the door.

Have you ever run into those people whose idea of a really swell time is fighting? Don't get pulled into their perverse form of entertainment. Say goodbye.

Along those same lines, when a person totally loses control and behaves like he has a permanent guest pass to the local loony bin, leave. Nobody wins under such crazy, irrational conditions.

Do you hate being lied to as much as I do? Nothing makes me lose respect more quickly for someone. This is another instance when I choose the "Goodbye Alternative."

These are just broad examples. The key is learning to trust yourself. You can do it. Pay attention to your body and the signals it sends your brain. It will never lead you astray.

Being Confident in Conflict

Psychological studies show that 85 percent of our joy and satisfaction in life comes from our interactions with other people. Only

15 percent is derived from sources such as achievement, success and material possessions. The better we are at handling those interactions, the happier we'll be.

Conflict needn't keep you up at night. You don't have to go through life with your stomach tied up in knots. Now you're a person who can deal with conflict confidently. You might not change people, but you can contend with them on equal terms. And what a freeing feeling that is! Enjoy it.

Step #6
Master Organization Politics

by Susan Dellinger, PhD

"Up and down the ladder it goes and where it stops... somebody *knows."*

Anonymous

All message sending and receiving takes place within a social setting — in this case, the business organization. The setting not only provides a background for the communications process, but influences who says what and how and to whom it is said. This chapter examines *institutional* methods of communication and the business organization as a social environment. Since you work and communicate within this environment, you must become more aware of the methods of receiving and sending messages and how they influence your management style. This style is very much dependent on the organization's management style: Who makes the decisions? Who has power, both formal and informal? What are the formal and informal communications networks? By virtue of sheer numbers alone, a business organization is enormously complex.

This makes it more difficult, but no less important, for a manager to analyze her organization in order to know how to play the corporate game.

Organizational Structure: The Hierarchy

American corporate structure has traditionally been a hierarchy, symbolized by a pyramid. Its prototype is the military, where a chain of command descends by rank from general to troops. The pyramid, with its ever-smaller and narrower layers, is a good illustration of this kind of hierarchy. The higher you are on the pyramid, the higher your status, and the fewer positions at that level. Each level is separated from the ones above and below it, and there is direct-line, linear reporting from level to level.

Such a hierarchy is even built right into almost every office building in the country. A few top-ranking executives have their offices on the top floor of the building. Each floor then descends by rank; the lowest-ranking and most numerous employees are found on the bottom floor (or even in some cases, underground). In these corporations, "climbing the corporate ladder" is no metaphor. When an individual is promoted, he or she moves up, physically, floor by floor, each climb in office location getting the individual closer and closer to the executive suite at the top of the building.

The organizational pyramid makes no bones about the way it distinguishes the Indians from the chiefs. Just to make sure, some organizations use titles to differentiate each level of status, and some even attach a numbering system to each title. Thus a first-line supervisor may be at Level 1. Salary and benefits would be scaled according to rank and number. Employees may not wear stars and bars to indicate rank, but they have no doubt where they stand. Status is symbolized not by stripes on their sleeves but by dress and office location, design, and furnishings.

However, dissatisfaction with the rigidity of the hierarchy has led to alternative organizational structures within the last decade or so. These are functionally based, rather than status-oriented structures, with workers divided into teams rather than ranks. A flattened rather than a tall organizational structure encourages more employee participation in an effort to motivate them to become more productive. Often, profit-sharing and incentive plans accompany flat structure/project-team types or organizations. These are largely experimental, but they may be prototypes of the future.

Communicating in the Hierarchy

Most of us still work in hierarchical organizations, and their structure defines the formal lines of communication that we must work with (or against). People who have worked in a hierarchical organization for any length of time will tell you that the strongest flow of information is in one direction — downward. The reason is simple: Your life on the job depends on understanding the messages from above. When an upper level "sends," you must be ready to receive.

However, since decision-making at the top of the pyramid is dependent upon information from below, many companies actively seek to improve upward communication. This isn't easy, for the larger the company, the more difficult it is to send a message up the line. This is true for several reasons. First of all, top managers generally feel that it is less important to listen to their subordinates than to their superiors. Not listening can be used as a status symbol. It is traditional for the person of higher status to talk and the lower status to listen. A superior can reinforce her status in her own eyes and the eyes of subordinates by interrupting them, changing the subject, and in general making it hard for them to get their messages through. Secondly, the "taller" the structure of the organization, the more levels the message must pass through to reach the top. Most organizations of any size have an active "filtering system" that acts to block or alter messages from below. The filtering system is usually most active at middle-management levels. It interferes with the flow of communications, making it much easier for information to travel downward through the filter than upward.

Executives and higher-level managers who remain unaware of the filtering process probably lose touch with the lower levels of their organizations. They may contract a major organizational disease: *executive isolation*. An organization suffering from this malady is in big trouble: The flow of communication is blocked and somehow must be reopened, or the organization will die. W. T. Grant Company, for example, which in 1975 experienced the biggest retailing failure ever, continued to open new stores while its old ones were losing money. New York headquarters either didn't know or didn't care to know what was going on in the field, and when new management tried to respond, it was too late.

In organizations where workers are unionized, a type of "end run" can be made around the blockage. Most managers agree that the union often receives information from the top more quickly than those at lower management levels. First-line supervisors often complain about this in statements such as, "If I want to know what's going on in the company, I ask my workers, not my boss." This happens because of top management's tendency to check out a new policy or major decision early with the union to avoid violating the current contractual agreement. While this procedure is logical, it means that management has told the union first, which makes the workers privy to the information before most of their own managers are. To the first-line supervisor, it represents an erosion of power and authority. Understandably enough, it's thoroughly resented.

Lateral communication, the exchange of information among those of relatively equal status in the hierarchy, also occurs within an organization. It is usually more effective than upward communication, but not as effective as downward flow because of the competition between employees on the same rungs of the organizational ladder. The very people who have the greatest opportunity and the greatest need to communicate (because they work together daily) often have the least motivation to do so. After all, you don't want to give away valuable information if you're not certain your coworkers will reciprocate. Ideally, the effective manager should practice active listening *on every level* of her organization. But in reality, the hierarchical structure makes this difficult. No matter how sharp your listening skills, the organization structure itself tends to block your use of them. Often people learn more from rumors than from official announcements.

Office Rumors as Communication

Rumors seem to be as much a part of the furnishings of an organization as the desks and chairs. In fact, they play a large part in group life. They are a means by which people cope with what they can't or won't understand, or with whatever is frightening them. Since people usually fear what they don't understand, often the two causes of rumor are one. Whatever is threatening or not understood creates anxiety; rumor dispels anxiety by seeming to explain things.

One of the strange aspects of rumor is that even an explanation that predicts some kind of disaster is preferred to no explanation at all. During the accident at the Three Mile Island nuclear power plant in Pennsylvania in 1979, rumors were flying that a nuclear meltdown was imminent. Whenever the public is alarmed, officials take to the airwaves to deny the rumors and give the "true" version. Whether or not they are believed depends on the officials' current credibility with the public. If the public believes that these officials have lied to them in the past, it reasons that they are likely to do so again and will refuse to believe their version.

The same holds true within the business organization. Whenever some change is in the air, the future becomes clouded. The change will undoubtedly affect people's jobs, but they don't know how. This uncertainty creates anxiety, so the rumor mills grind overtime. Whether or not the employees believe the organization's attempt to dispel the rumor depends on top management's record of credibility with employees. If it is low, no amount of official denying will dispel the rumors.

However, potential change and the organization's credibility aren't the only factors in the persistence and spread of rumors. Anxious individuals tend to believe and spread rumors much more readily than calm ones. In times of economic uncertainty, a great many employees are likely to be anxious and, therefore, rumor-prone. Combine large numbers of anxious people in an organization with a low-credibility management and you have the perfect climate for rumors. Rumors are like mushrooms; they grow best in the dark. An organization that has an atmosphere of super-secrecy, where all planning is very hush-hush and nobody is allowed to talk until the "president makes the official announcement," will have a flourishing rumor industry within its corridors.

Anything that touches people's lives will give rise to rumors, but most rumors in organizations are relatively short-lived: from the time a new boss takes over until people get to know her and know what to expect; from the time a new job is created until somebody fills it; from the time a move is contemplated until it actually takes place. If management vacillates or a decision is delayed, rumors will last that much longer. When something is actually happening rather than being anticipated, interest in rumors dies — until next time.

Rumors are often self-serving, reinforcing people's vanities and prejudices. When a promotion is in the offing, not everyone will make it, so it's more comforting to blame equal opportunity laws: "He only got the job because he's black" or ". . . because she's a woman" is easier to accept than the idea that he or she is more competent.

Real life is often tentative, ambiguous, and dull; rumors enliven the workday world. Unlike real life, rumors have well-defined plots. They improve on real life by assigning motives to the characters, embellishing the actions and, frequently, by bringing the story to completion. Although largely a myth, women are often still accused of being the rumor "mongers" within our companies. What are women to do to dispel this myth?

Golf With the Boss: Informal Networks

People like to *know*, and in the absence of authoritative information, they will seek out other sources, particularly about decisions that will directly affect their own work. *The more an organization insists on using formal lines of reporting, the greater the likelihood that an informal communication network will emerge.*

When organizations adhere strictly to formal lines, information often reaches employees too little and too late. Just as the Navy has its scuttlebutt, every organization has its grapevine. When a particular grapevine becomes reliable, it then functions as an informal informational network. One of the key differences between formal and informal communications networks is that the formal follows the hierarchical structure, while the informal does not.

For many reasons, people within an organization have friends on different levels of the hierarchy. A middle manager, particularly one who has spent many years in an organization, may have friends on several levels above and below. She has crossed paths over the years with a variety of individuals. Perhaps they have worked together and then were promoted or moved on, but they still maintain some channels of communication with each other. Such an interconnecting chain can send messages through an organization with lightning speed.

A manager with multiple sources of information has a great advantage in terms of information power. Eventually, as people are added to the group she's in touch with, a viable second communication network is formed, and this can be a powerful force in an organization. There are three basic requirements for a solid informal network:

1. It should be able to tap into employees on all levels of the organization. (At least one member must be part of the top management team.)

2. Unlike the formal network, it is built on an attitude of personal trust. Thus it has a more solid foundation than the formal network. In order to keep going, there must be a shared agreement within the network that each member will be responsible for passing on information quickly and accurately.

3. It does not spread "rumors." Its information is primarily factual.

The larger and more hierarchical your organization, the stronger the possibility that an informal network is alive and functioning within it. For years, skillful managers have used these informal systems to their advantage. They just "happen" to know things before they occur, or they make good "guesses" about what's going on. How? They've had advance warning. That's exactly what an informal communication network is: an early warning system.

In fact, more than one informal network may exist within the same organization. Several may be broad and multilevel: The operating vice president and all of her former plant personnel now scattered throughout the company, for instance, or that male social clique that does indeed play golf with the president. In addition, often smaller informal networks operate within individual departments and sections. It may be useful for a manager to be able to tap into more than one network in order to receive different types of information. How's your golf game?

A note of caution. Informal networks have been in existence for a long time. In fact, people who were once managers may be top executives now because they tapped into the right informal networks. Not only may they be aware of the networks' existence, but they may sometimes use the networks to test their organization. Occasionally, incorrect information is deliberately sent just to get a reaction in a problem situation. Thus you must be cautious and analytical about the information that you pass on.

The network should never be used to gain status. Although you may gain temporarily, you risk losing credibility if the information is incorrect. These networks would quickly lose their effectiveness if they turned into rumor mills. People are often subtly dropped from informal networks because they passed on information in order to make themselves look good (e.g., by seeming "in the know" or "knowing people in high places").

It is characteristic of a powerful, informal network that it is the information flow, not the sender, that's important. Informal networks work best when the higher-level sources of the information are never revealed and when the information is accurate.

Office Turfs

All humans have places and possessions that they regard as "theirs," even if they are not the legal owners. Whether it's a church pew or a park bench, anyone who sits in the same seat regularly comes to think of it as his or hers. The cook's kitchen, Archie Bunker's chair, the gang's back alley, the teacher's classroom, the home team's playing field are all examples of "turfs." A work group may take over a break room by occupying and using it regularly so that other groups come to think of it as "theirs," not "ours."

Robert Sommer, a researcher who devoted a great deal of time to the study of dominance and territoriality in mental institutions, found that each hospital had a well-established dominance hierarchy, each with its assigned space. Not only patients, but nurses and attendants were uncomfortable when Sommer, a doctor, sat down next to a patient in the day room. That was the patients' space, just as the nurses' stations belonged to the nurses.

A corner office may have become a "power position" (to quote Michael Korda) because corner positions are best for seeing what goes on and thus are easiest to defend. Where, for instance, would you sit in a large restaurant if you wanted to see who entered and left? Probably at a corner table with your back to the wall, facing the entrance. When seated at a table, the corner position is the easiest to defend from intruders.

A pair of social scientists have distinguished four types of territories in human societies:

1. Public, with free access, such as parks, streets, lobbies.
2. Home territories, with public access controlled by a group, such as a local bar or hangout, some workplace lunchrooms.
3. Interactional, a setting for people to interact socially, such as a break room, lounge.
4. Personal, controlled by an individual, such as a desk or private room or office.

Some spaces may serve a dual purpose. For example, two people in an elevator (public) may be engaged in an interchange of information (interactional). A company's real commitment to communication often can be gauged by the amount of space it makes available for interaction; if there is not enough space, public areas will be pressed into service — halls, elevators, restrooms.

The need for neutral or interactional space is often felt most acutely when differences need to be ironed out or policies negotiated, since people acting within their home territories have a built-in advantage (as the home team does in ball games). Why else does your boss call you into *her* office for a talk? Social scientists who wanted to put this idea to the test had student lawyers, one of the pair representing the prosecutor and one representing a defendant, negotiate a plea bargain in their respective dormitory rooms to see if the student was able to get better terms for his client when in his own dormitory. He was.

Another test of a company's people-orientation is how it handles the need for privacy. When people are crowded together and can't get away from each other, they will often get away by "cocooning," or retreating into themselves. Needless to say, this behavior discourages informal communications. Where do you go when you need to withdraw and think — away from ringing phones and constant interruption from other people? Some managers have literally nowhere to go to get away from their charges except the restroom.

Does your company permit employees to have personal territory that they control, such as a desk or wall space that they can personalize with pictures, plants, signs, or posters? (The company that forbids this is telling its people something — that this space is not really theirs.) Do employees have privacy, or are all the desks out in the open so that you have to counsel a worker in full view (and possibly hearing) of everyone else? Even if no one else can hear, the fear of the possibility of being overheard will stifle communication.

The open office in which every desk can be seen at once, rather than being democratic, is the exact opposite. An autocratic management that doesn't trust its employees has arranged to have them watched. Even in open offices, people will still stake out individual and group territories, but the markers will be more subtle. A softened plan, the office "landscape" with movable partitions and greenery, gives lower-echelon people privacy, but sometimes takes it away from middle managers and supervisors, who resent it.

What Sommer calls "hard architecture" — the bureaucratic or hierarchical building — is one in which everything has its place; people as well as things are kept apart. It attempts to ensure that all interactions will follow strictly prescribed patterns by restricting the movement of people, "keeping them in their place." Within it, communication is discouraged, except the messages that come down from the top through "correct channels."

Management Styles: What Makes a Winning Team?

Are you a task-oriented or a people-oriented manager? How did you get that way? Can you tell from your organization's style how your own style developed and perhaps why you are sometimes forced to manage in ways that make you uncomfortable?

Each organization is a system with its own rules, checks and balances, and priorities that govern the way the company functions. In other words, each organization has its own style. Our discussion of corporate style is an adaptation of the "four-system theory" of Rensis Likert and Associates of the Institute of Social Research in Ann Arbor, Michigan.

System 1 is just about identical with the hierarchical military model that developed out of 19th century needs. At the other end of the scale is System 4, which has no real counterpart (or very few) in today's business world. Systems 1 and 2 cover the majority of all companies today, and I will briefly describe System 4 as an instructive comparison. Each system also has its own type of managerial office layout (shown at the end of this chapter).

System 1 Organizations
1. High task and production orientation.
2. Devaluing of the workers and the needs of the people.
3. Strong emphasis on rules and regulations.
4. Use of punishment, threats, and fear to make people produce.
5. Strong maintenance of the hierarchical structure and direct-line reporting.
6. Decision-making and vital information hoarded at the top.
7. Communication almost exclusively downward.
8. Authoritarian and autocratic leadership style starting at the executive level and copied throughout the organization.

System 1 organizations seem to ignore the needs of people and the organization's responsibility to its workers. Organizations that continue to operate this way are probably much less productive than other types. Often, they are characterized by a high degree of white-collar turnover, low productivity, strong unions, strong informal informational networks, large amounts of overtime, and inadequate break rooms and leisure-time facilities. The average age of employees is over 40, and there are few minorities or women in the managerial ranks.

Although System 1 organizations break with most modern ideas about how organizations should be operated, it appears that at least *one-third* of American companies are closer to System 1 than to any of the others. Part of the reason for this is simply inertia: The larger the organization, the more deeply embedded is the organizational style.

Even in less rigid organizations, there are pockets of the System 1 style — certain departments, certain job functions, certain members of top management who are still living in the "good old days." They may produce some short-term results, but they will be largely unsuccessful in the long run. These System 1 pockets must either adapt to new modes or decline.

System 2 Organizations

1. Attempt to soften the emphasis on product and task-orientation and promote people-orientation.
2. Strong emphasis on improving working conditions, salary, and benefits; addition of "human relations" training so that managers can understand the needs of employees.
3. Maintenance of rules, yet selective "bending" occurs.
4. Widespread manipulation of employees through use of inducements such as promised advancement and glossy "public relations" recognition of good performance.
5. Maintenance of hierarchy, but with increased knowledge and ability of top management to tap into informal networks.
6. Decision-making still primarily at the top, but some minor decisions delegated downward (often characterized by titular department heads with responsibility but little authority).
7. Communication flow primarily downward with some new projects introduced to encourage some upward flow.
8. Leadership style quasi-democratic with emphasis on paternalism.

As organizations become more concerned with their employees — sometimes as a result of the pressure of unions or government agencies — some respond by moving toward a System 2 approach. However, unless you're fairly high up, System 2 is not much better to work in than System 1. At least System 1 is direct, honest, and standardized; if you break the rules, you're punished, and that's that. But System 2 organizations often cajole their employees into believing that they have a say in their work lives, when in reality they don't.

A typical example of System 2 behavior is placing individualized thermostats in every department. Since, of course, no two people can agree on a comfortable temperature, the wall thermostats are dummies. The real thermostats are hidden in the ceiling and centrally controlled.

Can a new carpet on the floor and increased medical and dental benefits buy happiness? Perhaps temporarily. Perhaps even some of the time for some of the people. At least with higher incomes and benefits, workers are freer to pursue happiness *outside* the job. But they may be no happier from nine to five than the System 1 employee.

You can probably click off numbers of male acquaintances and coworkers who fit into the following description of an average employee in a System 2 organization:

Good Old Joe

Joe has been working for XYZ Manufacturing for ten years. He's thirty-five years old and has been a second-line supply manager for four years. He topped out in the salary range last year and takes home a comfortable salary of $40,000, in addition to the full insurance benefits provided by the company. He's even invested in the stock plan and now feels that he owns a piece of XYZ.

Joe isn't an outstanding manager, but he treats his coworkers well. They meet most of the deadlines and generally provide a fair day's work for a fair day's pay. Joe's boss keeps encouraging him to "hang in there," his time for a promotion will come. But it's beginning to look less promising.

About a year ago Joe and his wife bought a sailboat with some money she had inherited, and now they take their two children out almost every weekend. Joe will also assume the presidency of his local Rotary Club next fall, he coaches one of the Little League baseball teams, and he's a valued member of the junior high school Parent Advisory Board.

He even mentioned to his wife that he was considering going into a second business with a friend of his. It wouldn't take much time, and after all, there's still some of that inheritance left. Besides, the family car will hold up for another year or two.

Does this example ring a bell? Would you promote Joe? How would you manage him? He's obviously got some talent that is untapped at XYZ and that he's redirected into other, outside activities.

This situation is a common one in American corporate life today, especially in System 2 organizations. Certainly the working conditions and salaries are great, but the real motivators are still missing — the excitement of doing interesting and challenging work, of growing and learning and "stretching" oneself to do even better.

System 3 Organizations
1. Marked increase in concern for employees.
2. Strong emphasis on evaluating the potential and interest of all employees so that they can be properly placed in interesting and challenging work; increased opportunities for movement within the organization, with both upward and lateral moves based on career paths designed by employees and assessment centers.
3. Company policy and rules used more as general guidelines.
4. Increased involvement of employees in decision-making and increased delegation of authority and responsibility.
5. General "softening" of the hierarchical structure, lessening of middle-management ranks, and emergence of project "teams" assigned to temporary job functions.
6. Decision-making pushed down to levels where the most information is available.
7. Strong *upward* flow of communication through attitude surveys, upward communication programs, viable suggestion plans, visible movement of top management among worker ranks in the field.

8. "Participative" leadership style, with employees encouraged to give input into decisions that will directly affect their jobs.

Although most organizations operate under System 2, some departments or pockets within them seem to approach the more people-oriented structures of System 3. System 3 is an attempt to adapt the corporate structure to tap the wealth of resources contained in its employees — because the productivity of the company's work force depends on it. A few isolated examples exist of whole companies operating under System 3. Harwood Manufacturing Company of Marion, Virginia, which has been frequently cited in recent management literature, began this system thirty years ago and has enjoyed increased growth and productivity ever since.

System 4: The Organization of the Future

1. Negation of the hierarchical structure; strong "team" management used.
2. Emphasis on *functional management*, rather than tasks or people. Work organized by function and projects which are constantly changing as the market and employees change.
3. Division of labor from boss/subordinates (management and workers) to project "teams" with a group of "equals" assigned to complete a project.
4. Emergence of the concept of "matrix teams." Individual jobs are determined by assignments to several different functional teams. An individual may work on several teams at one time.
5. High value is placed on worker autonomy and initiative: The individual employee charts her own "career path," sets her own goals, and becomes a full partner in decisions which result from project "teams."
6. Standardized corporate rules and policy are minimal. Employees set their own standards, operate on flexible hours, evaluate team members' contributions to the effort, share in the profits of the organization on the basis of the contribution of their team.
7. Decision-making is relatively equally shared throughout the organization. Top management's function is largely one of

long-range planning for the corporation as a whole.

8. Communication flow within the organization is excellent, particularly laterally. Due to the elimination of pyramid concepts, upward and downward communication is much less applicable.

Changing Your Organization's Style

Which office-arrangement diagram is most like your own? Do you like it? Is it making you more effective or hindering you? Which of the organizational systems is your company like?

If System 4 sounds ideal, it's still a long way off for most of us. How can we get there, assuming that we want to? Some changes must be initiated by top management, but there are other changes that you could make to bring about a healthier work environment.

1. *Know what your employees need and want.* The desires of most of today's employees were aptly summed up in a 1973 *Work in America* article:

> What the workers want most, as more than 200 studies in the past 20 years show, is to become masters of their immediate environments and to feel that their work and they themselves are important — the twin ingredients of self-esteem. Workers recognize that some of the dirty jobs can be transformed only into merely tolerable, but the most oppressive features of work are felt to be meaningless tasks, constant supervision and coercion, lack of variety, monotony, and isolation — all avoidable. An increasing number of workers want more autonomy in tackling their tasks, greater opportunity for increasing their skills, rewards that are directly connected to the intrinsic aspects of work, and greater participation in the design of work and formulation of their tasks.

2. *Listen to the ideas and input of employees* on all levels in order to encourage the upward flow of communication. What can you do to open the channels above you? If it is within your power, insist that executives get out of the office and start getting to know the work force. Have them visit areas over which they have no authority. If you use attitude surveys, report the findings

to employees honestly and ask *them* for solutions to the problems identified.

3. *Encourage lateral communication* by working more closely with your own colleagues. Find ways to get people together informally and to promote more interchange of ideas. Are there people on your own level whom you have been excluding? Their input could be valuable.

4. *Stop believing that power and status are derived from title and position.* Real power is earned by the esteem of people who trust and respect you, as you trust and respect them.

5. *Look hard at the real needs of people.* Don't attempt to placate employees with new carpeting and other "improvements." Is the work you ask them to do mundane, routine, boring? Can any jobs be restructured? Can some of your own tasks be delegated? Can you include them in more decision-making? Can any people who are no longer challenged by their jobs be moved laterally?

6. *Be receptive to new ideas and change.* Place high value on education and individual growth for yourself and your employees. Try to encourage your coworkers and your company to look for and adopt new ideas, and you do the same. Be willing to "risk."

7. *Take a close look at your organizational structure.* Are there departments reporting to you that are top heavy or individuals performing functions that are no longer needed? Analyze functions to be performed rather than departments to be staffed. If it is within your power, consider project teams. Does the space you are using help or hinder the changes you want to make? Could you make the physical setting more responsive to yours and other people's needs?

This chapter, and the exercises below, provide a means of analyzing your and your company's management styles. Once your analysis is complete, you may find a discrepancy between your own management style and that of your organization. You may want to adjust, or you may decide to make some changes within your own areas of responsibility. Good managers earn respect through use of effective management techniques.

Exercises

1. Make a drawing of your organization's structure from the president down through the employees according to job titles. (Your personnel department may have a list.) Which is the structure more like — the traditional pyramid-type hierarchy or the flatter, project team approach?

2. Analyze the *downward* communication flow in your organization as follows:

a. Take the organizational chart that you just made and see how many *names* you can fill in. Did you include all executives and everyone to and including your own level? How many could you identify by name below you? Were you more familiar with certain departments?

b. In order to check the effectiveness of your company's downward flow, identify an announcement of some importance that was made within the last month. Next, identify the people on the lower levels whom you have occasion to talk to. The next time you see them, ask them if they know about this announcement. See if they fully understand it.

c. In order to "check yourself," do the same with your own direct reports. Choose something you told them about a month ago, and see if they got it.

3. Analyze the *upward* communication flow:

a. Choose an issue, project, or report that you would like to bring to the attention of your executive(s). What form of communication would you choose? How would you know if you were successful?

b. Identify something that one of the people who report to you has done that you feel is excellent. Devise a method of bringing it to the attention of your top executives. See how successful it is. Remember, good management involves getting appropriate recognition for the performance of employees.

4. To analyze the *lateral* communication flow:

a. Select a few key people in positions equivalent to your own (peer level) and pick a piece of new, interesting information to pass on to them. See where the information travels, how fast, and with what accuracy. Try to determine what path it took — who added to it, changed it, and so forth. Did it get to any higher-level managers or executives? If so, what was its route?

b. The exercise for lateral communication flow is also a good one for determining the informal communication network. Who was involved in the spread of the information? Could you have predicted it? Do these people have an informal network in your company? If so, can you tap into it and use it to your advantage again?

5. Using your original organizational chart, play a game of "connect the dots," by connecting the names that you feel form an informal communication network in your company. Is there more than one? If so, use more than one color and identify as many as you can. See how far *up* and how far *down* each goes with the organization.

6. Answer the following questions about your company, about your department, and about the group you supervise:

Do most people seem concerned with just keeping their jobs?

Do most people enjoy their work and think that it is interesting and challenging?

When people do an outstanding job, are they usually rewarded with money, better working conditions, or a day off? Is your own boss told when one of your people does an outstanding job?

Is there any real opportunity to move up, to get a promotion?

Is management generally more concerned with getting the work out than with the contributions and needs of the individual employees?

Are people less concerned with good teamwork and more with making themselves look good?

Is the leadership fairly traditional? Is most of the decision-making done at the top?

Is it difficult for someone to get a message to a manager or executive? Can your staff speak freely with you?

7. If you have identified some management or communication problems in your company or department, is there anything *you*

could do to correct them? The place to start is with your own work group. Ask the people who report to you for their ideas. Talk with your boss and get advice. The changes you make for the better will not only help you and your people, but the entire company!

Office Layout For System 1

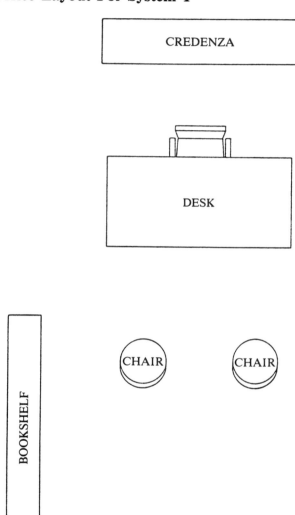

System 1 office layout: Desk is in the central position in the room. Guest chairs are positioned across from the desk and at some distance from it. Environment is generally sterile and the furniture quality and style are determined by position in the hierarchy.

Office Layout For System 2

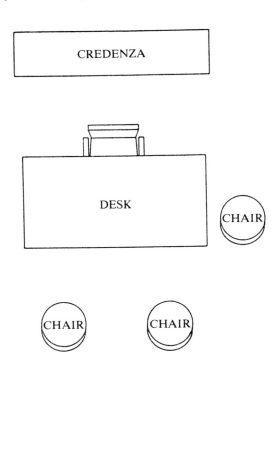

System 2 office layout: Desk is slightly off center but still the predominant piece. Guest chairs are closer to the boss and one is adjacent to her. Environment remains generally sterile with a few "softeners" such as plants and wall hangings.

Office Layout For System 3

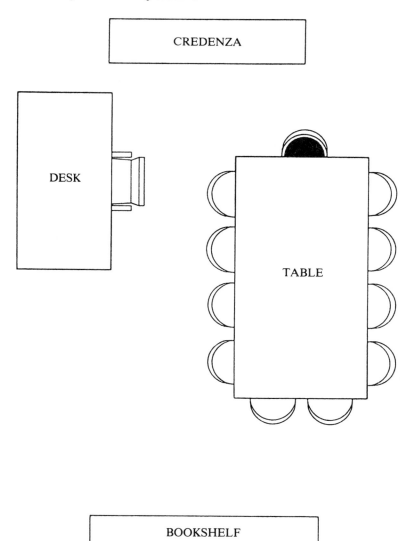

System 3 office layout: Desk is moved out of central focal position. Table is added, but it is generally a rectangular shape. The boss usually sits at position of authority at the table. Decorations will be similar to System 2.

Office Layout For System 4

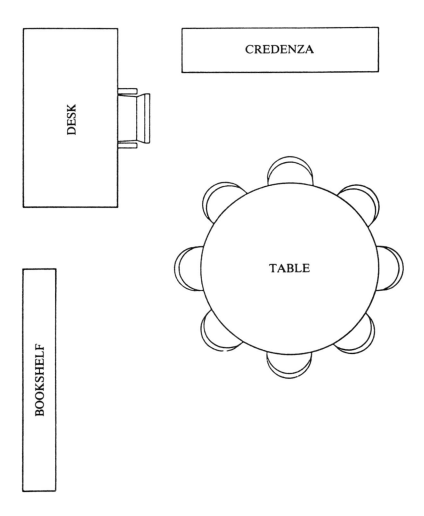

System 4 office layout: Desk is in the most non-predominant position in the room. The boss's back is to the door, indicating trust. Table is circular, encouraging equal participation. The arrangement of chairs forces the boss to converse around the table or, if she is seated at the desk, to turn and face the table.

Step #7
Negotiate With Skill

by Helga A. Rhode, PsyD

Being a competent negotiator is a powerful way to exercise greater influence over events in your work life. While not everything is negotiable, there are far more opportunities than many of us realize. Any time you are in a situation in which you and another person have conflicting interests, the potential for negotiation exists.

Because negotiation opportunities arise from conflict, it is important to view conflict as a chance to move toward positive change. With that attitude, you will be in a position to make the change work to your benefit.

When conflict happens, it often seems that the result will be a no-win outcome: either you tread softly and give in for the sake of the relationship, or you play hardball and make an enemy.

If you tend to be a softie, your stance in negotiations is one of making sure that no one gets upset. Your goal is to reach an agreement regardless of the cost. Your proposals are presented tentatively, you yield to pressure and you end up agreeing to a deal you later regret.

If you're more hard-nosed, your goal is to win at all costs. Your manner is demanding, you distrust everything the other person says, you use pressure tactics and you lie about your bottom line. You either end up getting what you want (plus an enemy for life), or not getting what you want (plus an enemy for life).

The alternative to either of these approaches is to negotiate for win-win consequences. The focus is on reaching an agreement which is fair and mutually acceptable. The process is based on reason, with proposals and counterproposals being judged on objective criteria. Yielding to pressure is out; yielding to principle is in. You end up with a change for the better and no one feels ripped off or manipulated.

Getting Ready

Before you actually enter into negotiations with another person, you must be perfectly clear about what you want and why you want it and have a range of options that will satisfy your interests. Begin your homework by asking yourself these six questions:

1. What do I want? Think in very specific terms about the kind of outcome you are after. For example, you may want a salary that is comparable to that paid for similar positions within the industry. Or you may insist on having a position that gives you opportunities to learn a new skill.

In cases where you are negotiating a change in others' behavior, beware of the temptation to state your wants in terms of what's wrong with what they're doing now. If you tell your supervisor that you don't want her to give you all the assignments that no one else wants, you risk being labeled a complainer. Concentrate instead on identifying one way that the status quo might be changed to improve your situation. How about "I want everyone to share equally in the grunt work"? Remember: unless your statement specifies something that is not happening now, you do not have a statement of what you want.

2. Why do I want it? Your answers to this question tell you what your underlying interests are. These interests are the criteria that must be met by any proposals made in the negotiations. If you're asking for a salary increase because you believe the pay rates in your department are inequitable, then *equity* is the criterion. Anything less would be an unacceptable compromise. But maybe what you're really after is recognition or status. By focusing on ends rather than means, you can begin thinking in terms of options rather than specific outcomes.

3. How can I get what I want? At this step in your preparation, you become a creative problem-solver. The process is one of brain-storming as many alternatives as possible that meet your criteria.

Let's see how creative you can be. Look at the puzzle below. See if you can connect all the dots with four straight lines without lifting your pencil from the paper. Give yourself at least 15 minutes before you look up the answer at the end of this chapter.

Brainstorming requires the same kind of unconventional think-ing that it takes to solve the puzzle. Win-win negotiations often require the same kind of creativity to make sure that no one loses.

Do a little brainstorming right now. Suppose that you have discovered that one of your underlying interests is "to feel valued." Receiving a salary increase is certainly one way people are made to feel valued. What are some others? A company car? An expense account? How many possibilities can you come up with? Three? Five? Twelve? Write down every option that comes to mind, no matter how absurd or ridiculous it may appear.

4. What are the most acceptable options? Obviously anything on your brainstorming list that is illegal or violates your moral code is out. Once these are eliminated, evaluate the others and circle those within the range of acceptability.

Give careful consideration to any option that might serve as a short-term solution in the event that your stronger, more dramatic proposals are rejected. Think about how some of the less desirable options might be combined to create a major change for the better. Would you be happy with occasional use of the company car if you also had stationery printed with your name and title?

The more options you bring to the negotiations, the better. This demonstrates your flexibility, as well as increasing the likelihood that you will end up with a win-win outcome.

5. What do I know about the other person? If your immediate answer is "nothing," you'd better get to work fast. Using the grapevine or direct personal contact, try to get some sense of what the other person's underlying interests might be. An excellent source of information is someone who has had experience negotiating with that same individual. The information you collect will enable you to tailor your proposals to address the other person's interests as well as your own. You can also plan for objections or refusals.

6. What's it like to be on the other side? Put yourself in the other person's shoes. Think what he/she might be thinking, feel what that individual might be feeling.

To make this easier, try "the other chair" technique. Put an empty chair facing you, then sit in it and pretend to be the other person talking to you (your vacated chair). Ask: "Why should I give you what you want? How much would it cost me? What benefits would I get in return? Would your requests satisfy or violate my interests?"

If you answer each question as honestly as you can, you will better understand your negotiating partner and be less likely to see that person as the enemy. You will also discover that you are unlikely to get what you want unless there is something in it for the other person as well.

Visualizing Success

One activity that will help develop a confident mind-set toward negotiation is borrowed from sports psychologists and behavior therapists.

Find a quiet place, sit or lie down, relax and close your eyes. In your mind, picture the physical setting where the negotiations will take place. See yourself acting calmly and confidently. Hear your voice as you offer your proposals in a firm, yet reasonable, manner. Visualize the other person listening attentively. Lastly, imagine the conclusion of a win-win negotiation and praise yourself for having done so well.

Conducting the Negotiation

Win-win negotiation includes six major phases. These phases may occur in a somewhat different order, or they may overlap or be repeated. Even so, they act as guidelines as you organize the discussion and serve to encourage the other person's maximum participation.

Phase One: Describe the problem. Draw on your preparation and state the problem or reason for the discussion as you see it. Be concise and objective. Beating around the bush or providing excessive detail sounds apologetic and will weaken your position.

Invite the other person to describe the situation from his or her perspective and make sure you understand.

Phase Two: Identify your interests. Explain what a negotiated agreement will do for you. Then ask the other side about its interests. Summarize the two sets of interests as criteria which must be met by any agreement that is made: "What we're looking for, then, is a way to provide me with more challenges in my work without disrupting the existing procedures for distributing assignments."

Phase Three: Brainstorm together. Invite the other person to add to the list of options you have prepared. Remember the ground rules: anything goes, and no criticism of suggestions until your ideas are exhausted.

This process can produce a feeling of partnership as you tackle the problem together. It also increases commitment to the final agreement because both of you have invested energy in working out a solution.

Phase Four: Evaluate options against interests. Review the list of options and assess their value in terms of your individual interests. Insist on win-win outcomes, even if it means interrupting the negotiations to allow time for more creative thinking.

Phase Five: Commit to a solution. At this point you consider the fairness or equity of a proposed agreement. The criteria used should be agreed upon by both parties. Market value, precedent, customary performance standards — any of these might serve as appropriate criteria.

Sometimes logic works, as in the case of a woman whose car was involved in a minor accident. Her insurance company directed her to a body shop 45 miles away. When she asked for a mileage allowance, she was told that company policy would not permit it. She calmly explained that the cost of the gasoline was an out-of-pocket expense incurred through no fault of her own, which neither she nor the insurance company could justify. The insurance company sent her a check.

Phase Six: Assign responsibility. Any agreement is only as good as the plans made for implementing it. Should a time limit be set? Do others need to be informed of the agreement? If so, who will do what by when?

Whether you request a written contract or settle for a handshake depends on your preferences and existing practice. The experts disagree on this point. Some say a written contract is worth only the paper it's written on; others believe a verbal agreement is worthless.

Whatever you choose, you are advised to write down the terms of your agreement, with or without signatures. Human memory is so faulty that a verbal agreement can quickly give rise to another conflict.

Increasing Your Effectiveness

Any time you communicate, two important variables come into play: what is said and how it is said — the content and the process. In negotiation, both content and process influence how the communication progresses, whether people treat each other with respect or whether tempers flare.

Consider win-lose bargaining. Your opponent digs in with the statement: "You will get a promotion over my dead body!" You react by feeling intimidated, angry, or defeated. You might reply, "Well, if that's how you feel, you can take your job and...!" The process in this interchange is aggressive and leads to a power struggle where one wins and one loses, or both lose.

In win-win negotiation the process is one of cooperation with both parties working together to remove the obstacle which interferes with a continued good relationship.

Communicate respect. When you give respect, you usually get it back. No matter how much you may resent or fear having to deal with a problem, your language and behavior should demonstrate empathy and politeness. The other person will find it much easier to hear what you have to say and the potential for agreement will increase.

View the person and the problem as separate. Refrain from attributing dishonest or harmful motives to the other person. Show genuine concern and a win-win attitude. Whether or not you like that individual sitting across from you is immaterial. Liking and fairness are separate issues. Your guidelines should be: logic, reason, diplomacy and tact. (The humorist's definition of tact is telling someone to go to hell and making him or her look forward to the trip.)

When you disagree, a simple "I see it another way" or "That hasn't been my experience" will make your position clear without provoking the anger that follows "you are wrong."

Remember that perceptions are personal. Each of us interprets the world in a slightly different way because we all have different life experiences.

When you negotiate, try to understand the other person's point of view. What appears to be stubbornness may only be a different vantage point. Above all, avoid getting into arguments about the rightness or wrongness of perceptions.

Listen actively. As listeners, we are able to process information coming in at a much faster rate than most people can put it out. Hence, there's a gap. In a conflict situation, we tend to use this extra time to focus on our anxiety or anger, or on planning our rebuttal. Active listening means that you use the gap to silently paraphrase and summarize what the other person is saying. Attend to the communication while disengaging your emotions. Only then will you be able to really hear the message and verify your understanding.

Ask open-ended questions. Questions that begin with "what," "when," "where," "why" and "how" facilitate communication and open the way to better understanding. "What" and "why" questions, in particular, can lead to mutual understanding of basic values and desires.

"Why do you feel I'm not ready for this promotion?" is a good example of how an open-ended question can get at underlying interests. If the answer is that you haven't had any experience preparing budgets, you can suggest that you're willing to take a training course or a night class.

Beware of using "why" questions as a form of punishment. "Why are you so stubborn?" will get you a defensive answer and worsen the relationship. It certainly won't enlighten you about the reason for withholding the promotion.

If you hear something that isn't absolutely clear, don't make assumptions. Ask questions.

Use skill in handling emotions. When feelings run high, people tend to act them out rather than talk about them. We shout rather than say "I'm mad!" We throw barbs and accusations rather than say "I'm jealous" or "I'm hurt."

One of the most powerful ways for you to exercise influence during a negotiation is to keep your emotions under control. Here are some guidelines:

1. Treat feelings as legitimate. Express both positive and negative emotions by owning them. Say "I'm glad" or "I'm mad," not "You make me mad." When you own the feeling, you are showing that you're in charge. Attributing your feelings to an outside source makes you come across as dependent or accusatory.

Acknowledge the other person's feelings with a statement such as "I can see how you might feel that way." That's not the same as saying "I'd feel the same if I were you." The difference is "I understand" vs. "I agree."

2. Don't get hooked by accusations. Defending yourself will distract you from your purpose of negotiating an agreement. Remember the saying about "sticks and stones." Doggedly focus on your goal and respond to accusations with "All right, that's how you see it, now how are we going to solve our problem?"

3. Let emotional outbursts run their course. In response to an outburst, stay silent, calm and confident. It doesn't matter whether the outburst is for real or is an intimidation tactic. If you offer no resistance, the temper tantrum will burn itself out.

Play fair. Never mind George Bernard Shaw's remark: "Don't do unto others as you would have them do unto you, because their tastes might be different." Playing one-upmanship or hitting below the belt will only lead to hostility.

Bluffs or threats might work at times. The problem is they are a gamble. If the bluff is uncovered, you look like a fraud. If the threat doesn't work, you have to implement what you promised and the only possible outcome is lose-lose.

The ultimate fairness in any negotiation is to insist on an agreement that is consistent with the parties' values and beliefs. If a suggested resolution conflicts with your underlying interests, say "no" and allow the other side to do the same.

Persist in seeking mutually acceptable solutions. Many negotiations end prematurely and unwisely because one or both parties become fatigued. Giving in because you're sick and tired will make you sorry later.

When you are overcome by irritation or frustration, stop and continue at another time. It's okay to say "I'm tired" or "I want to think things over." Sleep on it or go for a walk. You might come up with an "aha" idea to break the deadlock.

Unwise agreements can also result because one person yields to pressure. If you feel you're being intimidated or subjected to pressure tactics, stop the action and shift to a discussion of what's happening. Insist on respectful, rational interaction. Try a statement like: "Threats and accusations will only increase our conflict. I would like for both of us to settle this matter amicably and fairly. Let's work together and get back to solving this problem together."

If the pressure is aimed at making you accept an agreement before you're ready, explain that you need time to mull things over. Don't give in to warnings such as "everything is at a standstill until you give me your decision." Point out that you will get back to them at a certain time, then follow through.

Summarize agreements. Reinforce each minor agreement that is reached. Small though they may be, they represent success that can breed further success. If you emphasize points of agreement by occasionally summarizing the discussion, you will create a "can do" atmosphere. Future obstacles won't seem nearly so insurmountable.

Begin and end with positives. When frustration and hostility threaten to take over, do the opposite of what you feel like doing — be polite. Find something positive to say or do. A friendly, sincere personal comment or a good handshake are powerful ways of letting the other person know that you are a fair and rational negotiator.

Operate on the Principle of Least Interest (PLI). Simply stated, the less you want something, the more negotiating power you have. Conversely, the more you want something, the less negotiating power you have.

In practice, if you have prepared yourself to accept more than one outcome — a salary increase *or* a company car *or* an expense account *or* a new job assignment — you are more likely to get satisfaction and far less likely to succumb to pressure from the other side.

The PLI is a very potent psychological tool. You may think of it as a way to manipulate the other party by feigning disinterest. When used appropriately, however, the PLI is based on *real* options which you are willing to implement.

Many successful negotiators claim that you should never start discussion of a deal you can't walk away from. Putting it more positively, any conflict situation can have one of three outcomes: (a) you accept the situation as it is and learn to live with it, (b) you negotiate a change, or (c) you leave. Your willingness to leave, whether you actually take such action or not, will increase your leverage to maximize power.

The Nonverbal Side of Negotiating

For a complete discussion of nonverbal communication, refer to Step #4, "Communicate with Power." A few key points deserve highlighting because of their importance to negotiation skills.

Make your face agree with your words. When you say something funny, smile or laugh. When your message is serious, look serious.

Pay attention with your eyes. Look at people's eyes when you talk to them. Otherwise, they might think you are anxious, untrustworthy or submissive.

Look confident and relaxed. Your posture and gestures, like your face, can leak information about what's going on inside you. If you appear relaxed but alert, you will exude an air of confidence. Alternate between leaning forward, sitting up straight and leaning back as you see fit. The other person's reaction will be your best guide.

Your gestures should only emphasize your words. Pointing your finger will be perceived as accusatory. Fidgeting makes you look bored or nervous.

Communicate self-confidence by "looking like you belong" without appearing pompous. Coming across as helpless or apologetic gives the other person permission to exercise control.

Sound convincing. Keep your voice at an audible, controlled level. Sound sincere and caring when you address the human issues. Sound serious and firm when you discuss problem issues. Vary your pitch to emphasize your words, but not to a theatrical extreme.

Set the scene. The physical environment where negotiations take place can influence your behavior and emotions. Let comfort and convenience be your guide. Your own office can give you the advantage of feeling personally powerful, but it may have the disadvantage of intimidating others. It's also harder for you to leave. The reverse holds true for you when you negotiate on someone else's turf.

The other person's office can be used to your advantage if you feel comfortable with that arrangement. Giving in on this point can make you look reasonable, friendly and confident. Conference rooms are more neutral.

If the choice of place becomes a point of contention, you are better off conceding to the other's preference and totally ignoring your surroundings.

Where you sit or stand can also influence the negotiation process. Side-by-side seating is more likely to produce a cooperative atmosphere than talking across a table or desk. It looks and feels like you and the other person are partners, mutually working on a solution to a shared problem.

A Final Word

Which of these statements identifies your understanding of negotiation?
   a. Negotiating is the art of cleverly, cunningly and shrewdly outmaneuvering the other party.
   b. Negotiating is an open, objective, respectful discussion directed at a win-win settlement of some matter.
If you chose (a), you have missed the point. If you chose (b) and you follow the strategies outlined in this chapter, you will win more often and develop a feeling of confidence that most human problems, whether large or small, can be settled to everyone's satisfaction.
   I wish you success with win-win negotiations!

Answer to the puzzle:

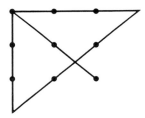

Further Reading

Cohen, Herb. *You Can Negotiate Anything.* Lyle Stuart, Inc., Secaucus, N.J., 1980.

Fisher, R. and Ury, W. *Getting To Yes.* Penguin Books, New York, N.Y., 1983.

Goddard, R. W. "Negotiating: How To Win By Forgetting About Winning." *Training.* March 1984.

Warschaw, Tessa Albert. *Winning By Negotiation.* Berkley Books, New York, N.Y., 1982.

Step #8
Make Persuasive Presentations

---

by Susan Dellinger, PhD

"Speeches are like the horns of a steer: a point here, a point there, with a lot of bull in between."

Anonymous

No doubt many business managers and potential managers and executives would prefer to appear before a firing squad than before a group to give an oral presentation. That's unfortunate, for while a firing squad is usually avoidable, giving an oral presentation is not. Whether the subject matter be zero-based budgeting, a strategic five-year plan, or some special project proposal, the oral presentation is frequently the means by which it is put before the company's decision-makers.

Formal presentations are becoming a way of life. Increasingly, top management must supervise departments and divisions that perform highly technical operations, the details of which they don't understand. As the work gets more complex and the number of divisions increases, understanding the details becomes impossible.

Indeed, understanding the details is not necessary, but understanding enough about the operations to make sound management decisions is. That's where the formal presentation comes in. Often, the formal presentation is the quickest way to impart necessary information to the decision-makers.

Presentation Preparation Checklist

1. Clarify your topic and your time allotment.
2. Analyze your audience.
3. Determine your objectives.
4. Select your material.
5. Organize your material.
6. Prepare audio-visual aids.
7. Control nervousness.
8. Practice.
9. Fine-tune your delivery skills.
10. Final preparations.

The formal presentation has great potential to influence the direction of the company. It must be succinct, accurate, and dynamic. Often, your potential as an executive may be evaluated partly on the basis of your ability to give a formal presentation. In the following pages, I will develop a blueprint for putting together an outstanding formal presentation, including how to prepare subject matter, audio-visuals, and *yourself*. I will also discuss the dynamics of the presentational situation — what to look for, how to respond to an audience and how to deal with the question and answer period.

Assume that you must make an important presentation to top management on a pet project. You have been given a date one month from now. Where do you begin? By preparing your material. The major source of your confidence when you give this presentation will be knowing that you are well prepared, and the key to this is through mastery of your material.

Given a month to prepare, the human thing to do is to put off the inevitable to a week or less before the presentation. But by doing that, you may omit or shortcut some of the important steps below. True, the tempo of your preparation should increase as you get closer to the date, with the last few days devoted to rehearsing and polishing. But begin the preparatory spadework *immediately*.

Step 1: Clarifying Your Topic and Your Time Allotment

Since the topic of presentations is often assigned by someone else, it is essential to understand exactly what you are expected to do. Ask clarifying questions such as, "Are there certain points, figures, or people, that you would like me to emphasize?" "How would you like me to introduce the topic?" "What's the most important point that you want me to make?" "Is there anything I need to know that you haven't mentioned yet?" Only when your topic is clear in your mind are you ready to proceed with preparing your material.

Most presentations to top management range from ten to thirty minutes; the average time allotted is around twenty minutes. After that, the presentor may entertain questions from the audience, the group may engage in informal discussion with each other and the presentor, or the presentor may be excused from the meeting.

Even though your central nervous system may prefer ten minutes to thirty, in reality *the shorter the time allotted, the more difficult the task*. It is much harder to be convincing in ten minutes than in thirty. With thirty minutes, you have leeway to read your audience, provide additional information, or just relax. If your presentation is important, ten minutes is cutting it close.

Contrary to popular opinion, you will have to almost double your preparation time for a short presentation. Whatever comments you make must be condensed to only the most relevant, powerful, and convincing. You will have to be *extremely selective*, and a lot of the supporting data will have to be abbreviated or eliminated. Unless you're careful, your presentation may seem choppy and even illogical. Each word will have to earn its pay. Of course, supporting data for your conclusions can be kept ready for the question period. At that time, your thorough preparation will enable you to back up and defend what you have said.

Step 2: Analyzing Your Audience

Before you open that file cabinet, before you ask your secretary to collect those figures, and certainly before you put in a requisition for slides to use for visual aids, sit down and *think* about your audience. Who are they? How can you successfully influence, impress, or convince them?

Unless you already know your audience well, you may need to gather some information about the people who will be evaluating your presentation. The following types of information may prove useful and could either make or break your presentation.

1. *Status*. Is your audience comprised of executives, managers, customers, clients, board members, peers? Do they have more status than you do? If the answer is yes, then the stakes for you are higher. (This is particularly true if these people have some degree of control over and influence on your career.)

You will want to present yourself to those of higher status in a way that is appropriate to a person on your level. I once knew a middle manager who blew a presentation to a group of his company's vice-presidents by asking them to consider his proposal at their Friday afternoon golf game. They resented his cavalier approach and felt his mention of it was presumptuous. In their minds, he had "forgotten his place." His proposal was rejected.

However, if you are of higher status than members of your audience, this presents other problems. You may be anxious because you feel that they are expecting great things from you. Whether or not this is true, you do not want to appear condescending, nor do you want to come across as arrogant and self-important. If you are overly concerned with yourself or with making a big impression on your audience, you will be less likely to succeed.

You could have an audience of people at various status levels, some higher and some lower than yourself. This will be a mixed blessing, because you will not be able to direct your presentation to any one level. But on the other hand, you'll probably be forced to deal with them as individuals. This is positive and should be one of your goals.

2. *Influence*. Your audience may be in positions to influence

those who have high status. Identify the relationships among people in the group. Who has influence over whom?

3. *Demographics*. In this category are age, sex, and background. You may want to slant your comments in a different way for a group of conservative executives than for a citizen's group composed of a cross section of the community.

Age and sex are only a part of it. Identifying the backgrounds can become a complex problem. What kinds of job histories do they have? I once knew a speaker who took a pot shot at truck drivers in her talk, only to find out later that one audience member owned a trucking company on the side. Religious and ethnic jokes can also backfire.

4. *Education*. An important part of audience background is its educational level. Does your audience speak your language? That is, does it share a technical education with you and thus a common vocabulary? If so, you have it made. If not, you will have to translate your jargon into *plain* language and use examples drawn from common experience. Otherwise, the audience will not understand you and you will fail, no matter how well you know your subject.

5. *Experience*. Education and experience are not necessarily comparable. Your audience may have a wealth of experience in your area, so be sure to deliver your presentation at the audience's level of understanding and expertise.

Of course, people in the audience may have more experience than you do. If so, you may want to clarify the reason why you were chosen to give this presentation. It may be that you can look at the subject from a different angle from theirs.

6. *Interests*. This includes both work interests and outside interests. For example, if you are presenting a new idea to a number of different departments, do you know the special problems and interests of those departments and how your idea will affect each one? What reasons might they have for being in favor of it or opposed to it? If you can't answer these questions, you could be in real trouble. All specialists tend to be myopic about their specialties, but top management needs to look at the entire picture. Talk to people in other departments and find out their problems and points of view.

Discovering the outside interests of your audience may require some digging. What are their hobbies, leisure activities, special concerns? You can establish rapport with your audience by referring to these interests. One successful speaker I know, when addressing the National Secretaries Association, took a potshot at the IBM Executive Model typewriter. With the local bankers, she referred to a controversial decision by the county commission that affected them. This kind of information about an audience can pay great dividends.

7. *Peculiarities.* Every audience is different. When you give the same presentation to more than one group, you quickly learn that what works with one group often doesn't work with another. Some remarks may be perfect for most groups, but offend another. When President Carter spoke in Mexico, he referred to "Montezuma's revenge," a well-known joke to North Americans but puzzling and insulting to Mexicans. One manager failed miserably in a presentation to managers of another department in his company because he told a slightly off-color joke to an audience that (unknown to him) was quite religious.

Of course, you will probably not be able to cover all the bases in the search for peculiarities in a particular group. It certainly doesn't hurt to ask someone who has spoken to or knows this group of people if there is anything you should avoid saying or doing. It could mean the difference between success or failure.

Few people can afford time for a thorough audience analysis. But if you have worked in your organization for a while, you probably have more resources than you think. Tap into one of those informal information networks, or stop and think about the information resources at your disposal.

Step 3: Clarifying Your Objectives

When you have firmly grasped the nature of your topic and audience, you will then need to firm up your objectives. Ask yourself, "Exactly what do I hope to accomplish with my presentation?"

In defining your objectives, there are three areas to consider:

1. *Information.* Do you want them to know something that

they don't know now? If so, your objective is to give your audience *information*.

2. *Attitude.* Do you want them to adopt a certain feeling about a project, yourself, your department, or your organization? If so, your objective is to affect the *attitude* of your audience.

3. *Action.* Do you want them to *do* something as the result of your presentation (e.g., increase the budget, extend the deadline)? If so, then your objective is to convince them that the action you propose is necessary and move them to do something about it.

So you want them either to know, to feel, or to do something, perhaps all three. And what specifically is that "something"? You'd better get it clear in your own mind or you'll never get it clear in theirs. Unless you know the result you're shooting for, your presentation will lack focus and direction. As the old saying goes, "If you don't know where you're going, you might end up somewhere else."

Once you know your objectives, *write them down* and check to see if they are (1) specific, (2) measurable, and (3) realistic. If they are specific, they will be phrased in concrete, active words. If they are not specific, come far enough down the abstraction ladder until they are. Even if your objectives are specific, they may not be measurable. In other words, how will you know that you have achieved them? Can you ask for a vote or get immediate oral or written feedback from the audience?

The third criterion is equally important: Are these objectives realistic? Have you bitten off more than you can chew? For example, can you realistically expect to accomplish a total overview of the two-year project wth additional projections for the next five years in a fifteen-minute presentation? If your reply is no, now is the time to redefine your objectives, limiting them to what you can realistically hope to accomplish.

At this point, you must also draw on what you have learned about your audience. What *can* you reasonably hope to accomplish with this group of people? If they are not the decision-makers, can you realistically ask them to take action on your proposal? Would it not be better to set objectives that would give them information about your proposal, and enlist their support so that they can then, in turn, influence the real decision-makers?

Step 4: Selecting Your Material

You have (1) clarified your topic, (2) analyzed your audience, and (3) set your specific objectives. Finally, you are ready to choose your material. Now is the time to be ruthless in applying the test of *relevance* to every piece of material that you consider. Only those items that relate specifically to your topic and will help you reach your objective with that particular audience can be included. Everything else — no mattter how fascinating you find it or how nice it would sound — must be ruled out.

Experienced speakers usually follow a logical process to determine what to include. Begin by brainstorming possible subtopics. Jot down ideas as they hit you. Don't interrupt the flow of ideas to criticize each one as you write it down. Now read back through the items and cross out any that are irrelevant. Read through the ones that are left. Have you forgotten anything? If so, add it to your list.

Now you are ready to think about the natural sequence and organization of the points you have written down. Look at the accompanying chart called *Methods of Organizing Material*. Each kind of material that you have will fit into one of these categories.

For example, if your proposal will accomplish some important gains for the company, each gain will be one of the "points" of your argument for it. (Method #3.) The points that you are making will need to be arranged in some kind of order. If points 1 and 2 must be understood before you can discuss point 3, then logically they must come first in your presentation. Or (especially if time is short and your audience impatient) you might begin with the most important point and follow with points in descending order of importance in case any have to be omitted. Or, if you want to lead your audience up to your most important point, you could reverse that order, saving your most important point for last.

When you have decided what you're going to do, go back through your list and number your points in the order in which you think you will present them and rearrange them in sequence. You now have a *rough outline.*

Review the outline and add a check mark next to the points that will require additional material. You have now arrived at the *information-gathering* stage. It's time to enlist the aid of your secretary in pulling files that contain specific figures, quotes, flow charts, or whatever else you think you will need.

Step 5: Organizing Your Material

Once you have collected most of the information and material that you think you will need, you are ready to take Lyndon Johnson's advice. The way in which you organize your information will be critical to the success of your presentation. Following the steps below should aid you in organizing:

1. Collect all the materials you have gathered on your desk in front of you. Get out your rough outline and *check off* the items that required additional information which you now have.

2. You are now ready to revise your rough outline. Prepare a second outline based on your additional research. You may have uncovered additional facts that will require a slightly different emphasis and hence a different organization. On getting further information, points that seemed important may now seem less so. Does the sequence seem right? Ask yourself, "What needs to come next? Should this item come before or after this statistic?"

3. Once you have completed the second outline (this is your real working outline), you are ready to consider an *opening* and a *closing* for your presentation. The following are some hints on effective openings and closings:

Openings

The all-important beginning moments of a presentation set the tone for the entire event. In classic public-speaking training, students were encouraged to use the "opening joke" technique. Unfortunately, this method became so stereotyped that these openings themselves became a joke — "A funny thing happened to me on the way to the speech tonight...ha, ha, ha...and now I would like to speak to you about capital punishment." Opening jokes often have nothing to do with the topic of the talk itself, and therefore they are pointless except to relax and warm up the audience. (They actually serve more to relax the *speaker*.) Waste no time getting into your subject with pointless jokes. Every minute counts. Your opening should accomplish all of the following:

1. Get the attention of the audience, so they are interested in two things — your topic and you.
2. Set a positive tone and establish rapport with your audience.
3. Be consistent with your topic in order to introduce it.
4. Allow you to present yourself as relaxed and in control.

Easier said than done? That is why you often spend more time trying to think of a good opening than in preparing the rest of the speech. A stereotypic salesman might get the attention of his audience with a peppy handshake, a flashy smile, and a glossy photo of his product. As a persuasive presenter, you might do it simply with an appealing presence and excellent delivery skills. But whatever you do, you must focus attention on yourself, and off the big board meeting that starts in an hour, that irate client on the telephone, or that cocktail party tonight for the Mayor. Otherwise all of your careful preparation will be wasted.

One good way to open is with an illustrative example or anecdote. It doesn't have to be funny; it *should* be about the topic. Perhaps an example of something specific that's happening in your industry will illustrate why you feel that your proposal has merit. The ideal anecdote is brief, memorable, and *to the point*.

Another way to open is to grab your audience's attention with a startling statistic ("Did you know that this company lost umpteen thousand manhours last year because of _____?") or a surprising statement ("Everybody seems to think that xyz's product lines are profitable. But my investigation shows that they're badly mistaken.") Or take a familiar saying and turn it around so that it becomes fresh and attention-getting ("If silence is golden, then the person who can lower the efficiency-killing decibel level here will make this company a mint."

Closings

An old, three-step speech-making axiom says, "Tell 'em what you're going to tell 'em; tell 'em; then tell 'em what you've told 'em." The last, a *summary*, is one method of closing a presentation, and often it's useful for a complex subject or one with a number of interrelated items. In case anybody's mind wandered while you were pursuing one of the items, a good summary reiterates and reminds your audience of the main point you want to leave them with. The last two or three sentences will be the *first thing* that the audience will remember about your presentation. Therefore, the closing, like the opening, must be carefully designed to help you accomplish your objectives with your particular audience. Ask yourself, "What can I say at the end that will really solidify my presentation, that will really make them know, believe, and act on my comments?"

To serve its purpose well, the closing must be powerful. You can't just come to a stop: You want a climax for your presentation, not a shutdown. And whatever you do, when you finish your closing, shut up and get off the stage, or move away from where you've been standing. Don't keep talking after your closing or you'll undo everything you've done.

NOTE: If a question and answer period is to follow, you may want to save some lucid or dramatic points or data to reveal here. If you have done your homework on audience analysis and have thoroughly researched your topic, you should be able to *predict* what questions will be asked. You should certainly give some thought to anticipated questions. And, if you have collected three times the amount of material than you can use, you will have plenty of back-up information for the question period. (Some speakers have been known to plant questions in the audience. Why not? In case no one else asks, those questions will not be overlooked.)

Step 6: Preparing Audio-Visual Aids

Too often, the novice begins working on a presentation by choosing visual aids: "Gee, I've got these great slides I could show!" The trouble with that approach is that you are likely to build the presentation around the slides instead of the other way around. Don't let the tail wag the dog. Only now, when you know what you are going to say, should you begin thinking about slides or other visuals to support your presentation.

You may have been jotting down notes to yourself on possible visual needs as you went along, but not until you have completely prepared your talk are you ready to decide what media aids could enhance it.

We do encourage you to use some visual support because sight is the most powerful sense — almost *six times* as powerful as the other four: sight, 75 percent; hearing, 13 percent; touch, 6 percent; smell, 3 percent; and taste, 3 percent.

What your audience sees will probably also be remembered better than what it hears. Many years ago, a young trainee had to give a practice speech at a management-training class. She slouched to the front of the room, stumbled up the platform, and dropped her notes and her glasses. Just as the audience was going numb with embarrassment, she announced her topic, "How Not to Give a Speech," the beginning of which she had just demonstrated, Now, twenty or more years later, no one remembers what she said, but they still talk about what they saw.

Carefully chosen visual aids will support and enhance your message. Some of the most helpful presentation aids are described below:

Flip chart. Probably the most widely used visual aid in business presentations, a flip chart is generally easily accessible, either as a built-in feature of most conference rooms or held on a portable easel. It can be prepared ahead of time and used spontaneously during your talk. If you are far enough away from he audience, you can even pencil notes to yourself on the borders, thus seeming to work without notes. Some hints for using a flip chart successfully include:

1. No more than ten words or figures per chart.
2. No more than 6 lines of information per chart.
3. Use a blank sheet between each sheet containing information so that the bottom one won't show through and be distracting.
4. Use tabs to separate different sections and for easy access as you manipulate the chart.
5. Practice your swing. (Swinging the top sheet over the back of the tripod can be tricky if you've never done it before.)

6. Use the last chart to summarize your major points.

Remember, the further away from you, the less some of your audience is going to be able to see. Check your chart from the back of your room for readability. For large gatherings, put less on each chart and make everything on it bigger.

Chalkboards. Most conference rooms are equipped with a chalkboard, the second most common visual aid. Like the flip chart, the chalkboard can be prepared ahead of time or used spontaneously. It has the added advantage of being erasable but the disadvantage of being messy (you could wind up with chalk dust all over your new suit). You also must turn your back on your audience as you write.

Cardboard aids. Similar to the flip chart, cardboard aids may be maps, charts, pictures, or outlines — anything you can put on a piece of cardboard with a stand-up backing. They can also be displayed on a flip-chart easel, taped on a chalkboard, or attached to a felt board (plywood covered with felt).

Handouts. Often, your presentation will include graphs, pictures, or complicated statistics that you would like your listeners to be able to take with them for future reference. A prepared handout can be passed around so that your audience will not have to take notes while you talk. Text as well as pictures can be used.

Handouts should be used with caution, however. Don't give out too much information or it will go unread, or (worse yet), the audience may begin to read while you're talking and you may never regain their attention. Never hand out anything that you don't have time to go over with your audience. "Go over," however, does not mean that you read the handout to them, which is insulting as well as boring. Instead, refer to the handout from time to time, i.e., "Now in the second paragraph, as you'll notice, the statistics show that..."

If you want to include line drawings, cartoons, graphs or even photographs, have your secretary type the printed material (preferably short and in outline form for easy comprehension) and paste the drawings or other visuals on the page exactly as you want them to appear on your finished handout. You now have camera-ready copy, which you can take either to your company's printing department or to a nearby quick-print shop to be duplicated. (Some shops may make color reproductions.) If you want to use attention-getting color inexpensively, you can have your handout printed on colored stock.

If you want to use larger print on your handout than you can get from a typewriter or if you are printing your own flip charts or cardboard aids, use transfer letters from art supply or office stationery shops.

Models and samples. It can be invaluable to show an audience a small scale re-creation (e.g., an architect's model of a building, piece of equipment, or hardware), provided that they can really see it. This means that the model must be placed where everybody in the audience can see it, or passed from hand to hand, or else the audience should be given time to walk up and examine it. Instead of a model, you might bring in an actual object to demonstrate; for instance, a new piece of equipment that the audience could inspect.

Slides. Over the last few years, the use of slides in formal business presentations has greatly increased. Not only do slides make your presentation more professional, they add interest and enable you to say more in fewer words. Many larger companies have sophisticated media departments that will produce them at minimal cost. You can also take your own 35 mm slides, buy ready-made slides, or have them made from any poster, picture, drawing, or graph. If your visual is black and white, you can introduce color by sandwiching a piece of colored gelatin between the slide and the slide mount.

Here are some hints on presenting slides with your presentation:
1. Avoid overkill. Too many slides can be just as boring as none at all.
2. Make each slide count. Use one for each major idea.
3. Make your slides work for you. Never tell your audience in detail what they can see for themselves. Let the picture convey the message.
4. Use color, if possible.
5. Make sure the pictures are of good quality. If the pictures are really not that good — out of focus, off-color, badly

composed — should you use them at all?

6. Intersperse pictures with words. Blend the two for more impact by combining other visual aids.
7. Have the equipment set up and ready to go long before you start.
8. Test the equipment and practice using it. Upside-down slides are embarrassing, and they waste valuable time while you reposition them in the projector.
9. Don't try to ad lib during your slide presentation. Plan what you will say during the slide presentation.
10. Position yourself in front of the screen. This is your show, not the projector's.
11. Don't turn out all the lights. Try to choose a room where you and the audience can be in the light with only the screen area in the dark.
12. Make at least your opening and closing comments with the projector off and lights on, bringing your audience's attention to you at the most important moments.
13. Don't let the slides dominate your entire presentation.

Film. Film is sometimes used in a business presentation, but it should be short. When you use film, you give up your control of the situation, and it may be difficult to regain the audience's attention. If you want to use a film, make sure it meets the following criteria:

1. Is it absolutely necessary to achieve your objectives?
2. Is the film professionally done? Informative? Interesting?
3. Is it current? No mini-skirts or '63 Oldsmobiles?
4. Is it short enough to allow you more than 50 percent of the time for your own comments?
5. Will it be new to your audience? (If the majority has seen it, simply referring to it might be enough.)
6. Will anything in it be controversial or offensive to your audience?
7. Does the film make unrelated points that will detract from your objectives?
8. Will the room provide comfortable viewing for everyone?
9. Will you be able to acquire the film, set up the necessary

equipment, and preview it before the presentation?

10. Will you be in violation of any copyright laws by showing the film?

Pointers on Visual Communication

How graphics look is very important. If your company has its own audiovisual department, printing facilities, or graphics designer, you may be able to receive some valuable help in designing and making your visual aids. Although the creation of many graphics is best left to artists and designers, you can produce an effective flip chart, cardboard aid, or handout by following these pointers:

1. *Readability is your primary aim.* For maximum readability, you need *few* design elements (words or pictures) per page, *big* elements and *simple* elements (no tricky drawings with details that can't be seen beyond the first row).

2. *Contrast design elements and background.* This is essential to readability at a distance. Black on white is an obvious choice. If you want to enliven your aid with color, researchers have discovered that yellow on black or white on black closely follows black letters on white ground in readability. Other acceptable choices are white on dark blue or dark green, green on white, and red on white, in that order. The poorest choices are green on red, yellow on white, and the reverse.

3. *Keep it neat and simple.* One or two colors, styles of type, or kinds of pictorial elements per page are plenty. The more diverse the elements, the more they compete with each other for your audience's attention. Each piece of your flip chart or cardboard aid should be about *one* thing only for maximum impact. A *unified* design — one in which the viewer's eye is drawn to the center of interest — can help achieve this.

4. *Balance the design.* Balance can be either *formal* or *informal.* An arrangement is formally balanced when every element on either side of an imaginary central line matches exactly. An arrangement is informally balanced when the elements on either side of the line have the same visual weight but do not match. Informal balance is more difficult to achieve. If in doubt, formal balance is always safe.

5. *Choose a lettering style that reinforces your message.* Thick,

boldface type gives an impression of strength. Gothic has an old-world flavor. Script is delicate. It would look absurd, for example, to use delicate script for heavy machinery when it's more suitable for a perfume advertisement.

No matter which visual aid you choose, always remember that *you* are the most important visual aid. What you do and how you behave is more important than any object that you use in your presentation.

Step 7: Controlling Nervousness

No matter how many beautiful visuals you have prepared and how many marvelous words you have written, your presentation will falter if you haven't prepared yourself both mentally and physically. To begin with, that uptight feeling, the butterflies in the stomach, are normal and even *healthy*. Most professional speakers still get nervous before an important speech. The reason is simple: It's important for them to do well, and that produces tension and starts the adrenalin flowing. Nervousness should be accepted as a natural phenomenon, and you can learn to make it work for you. There are both physical and mental ways to channel this extra energy.

Physical control. Take deep breaths before and during your presentation and relax your muscles. Walk around before you enter the room, sit in a relaxed position while you wait to go on, and do some isometric exercises at the table (such as pushing against the table with your hands and releasing). You should also prepare your voice beforehand. Try to talk to someone before you stand up.

When you are about to begin, place your feet comfortably apart to balance your weight. Then begin to build some movement into your presentation. Walk over to your visual rostrum. (However, don't pace because that is distracting.)

Mental control. Of all things, the most important are to be prepared and to be confident. If you have done your homework and practiced your presentation, your self-confidence should bolster you against your nervousness. Nobody else in the room has done the amount of preparation that you have. During the time that you are in front of the audience, *you* are the expert. Assume that the audience supports you. Why shouldn't they? It is a rare audience that does not want a speaker to succeed. They want to have a pleasant, positive experience as much as you do.

Never admit your nervousness to an audience, even jokingly. Interestingly enough, even an audience that knows you is rarely aware of the degree to which you are nervous. If you call attention to your nervousness, however, the audience will begin to look for observable signs of it and soon will stop listening. Then it will be difficult to recapture their attention.

The most helpful thing you can do during the presentation is to concentrate all your attention on your audience. Think about them and you will begin to forget about yourself. This will almost automatically establish rapport with the audience. If your message is *receiver-oriented*, you have already put your audience first. You know what you want to say, you believe it's important, you've worked hard at putting it into a format that your audience can understand. Now think about how much *they* are going to benefit from understanding it and you'll be too busy to worry about yourself. If you put the audience first, you must succeed!

Step 8: Practicing

People who deliver a great number of formal presentations will tell you that it is very important to practice, practice, and practice some more The more you rehearse your presentation, the more confidence you will build, and the fewer surprises you will have on stage. In addition, not only will your mind learn the content of your talk, your body will also get used to the rhythms.

Try the following system for practicing your presentation. It has worked for many people who were learning to develop their one-to-group skills; see how it works for you.

1. Speak your presentation (using your working outline) into a *tape recorder*. Then play it back and analyze it carefully. Look for logical flow, correct language and grammar, transitions, effective opening and closing. (*Note:* Don't pay much attention to how your voice sounds. Most tape recorders distort voices. In fact, pretend

you are listening to someone else. It may help you be more critical.)

2. Add the visual impact of your delivery by rehearsing the entire presentation *in front of a mirror*. Do this two or three times. Take particular notice of how you *look*. What does your body do? Are you gesturing naturally? Are you using facial expression? Do you like what you see? If so, remember it. If not, change it. Now is the time.

3. After you have practiced your presentation on tape and standing up in front of a mirror, you are ready to do it in front of a live audience. Ask a friend or two to come and listen to you. Tell them you'd like to do a dry run and you want constructive criticism. I knew a woman who, after blowing an important presentation, felt bewildered because her husband had said her rehearsal was such a success. Choose someone who will not only give you constructive feedback, but who will be part of your audience or who knows what the presentation is about.

4. Practice your presentation in the *actual environment* where you will give it. Also, incorporate any *visuals* that you will be using. Again, this will eliminate the surprises, such as not knowing where the electrical outlets for the projector are or finding the rostrum too high.

Step 9: Fine-Tuning Your Delivery Skills

During the practice period, you will not only be fine-tuning your presentation itself — you should be working on your delivery skills as well. When you use the tape recorder, pay attention to your wording. When you practice in front of the mirror, pay attention to your body language. When you rehearse in front of people, you should become more aware of eye contact, voice inflection, and timing. When you incorporate visual aids, practice until you handle them smoothly and efficiently.

The delivery of your presentation is equally as important as the content. Many speakers are skilled in the area of delivery, but audiences often leave wondering exactly what they said. On the other hand, some speakers are expert in their field but have great difficulty in getting it across to others. You will be more confident if you have carefully prepared your content *and* your delivery.

Wording. Spoken English is obviously different from written English. People often do not speak in complete sentences. The following has been transcribed literally from a tape recording made during an interview: "I'm from New Jersey and I find when I was up there — and my friends who are still up in the north, when they look at Florida they think of Disney World and Circus World and Sea World, but we don't have much in the way of culture — according to them."

This is grammatically incoherent in print, but it's not incoherent to the listener. Nor is this example unusual. (The speaker was a college professor, and almost everyone speaks this way informally.) I am not suggesting that you take the example above as a model for your speech. I merely use it to make the point that you cannot prepare a speech as you would prepare a written paper. For a written paper, the sentence is the unit you will be working with. But for a speech, *the unit is the phrase.* Work with phrases; they sound like natural speech.

Your language should be conversational, direct, and simple. Avoid long, involved sentences. Avoid jargon: if even one person in your audience may not understand a term, either define it or don't use it. Practice pronouncing any words you have difficulty with or, better yet, replace them.

Body movement. Stand erect at all times. Place your feet firmly on the floor about a foot apart. When you walk, stride naturally. Taking very small steps is generally a sign of nervousness.

Gesture. Try to be natural. Some people are more naturally demonstrative than others, so if you are not a person who "talks with your hands," don't try to. Also, don't become stiff by keeping your hands in your pockets, clasped behind you, or gripping the podium, pointer or chalk. Let your hands fall freely by your sides, or rest them casually on the rostrum.

Facial expression. Most of the audience will be looking directly at your face. Although a deadpan expression may work for playing poker, it is usually not effective when giving a presentation. Audiences prefer speakers who are animated because they are more interesting. And don't forget to smile. It's a rare audience that doesn't appreciate a friendly smile on the face of a speaker.

Eye contact. The importance of establishing firm eye contact with the audience cannot be exaggerated. Just as we assume negative things about someone who drops their eyes in conversation, the same is true of a presentor. *You must look at your audience.*

Here are a few hints concerning eye contact in presentational speaking:

1. At the beginning and end of your presentation, pause and look out at your audience for four or five seconds. This will demonstrate your command of the situation and give the audience a chance to absorb you visually before you begin to speak.

2. Do not *read* your presentation at any point. This automatically breaks eye contact with your audience. If you *have* to read something, be sure this part of your presentation comes after you've had a chance to build rapport with the audience. Reestablish eye contact with your audience frequently as you read.

3. When using visuals, do not talk to the flip chart or the slide screen. Memorize the content so that you can face the audience when explaining it.

4. Maintain eye contact with your audience throughout your presentation. (If you are concentrating on the audience, this will occur naturally.)

5. Choose three or four people from different parts of the room to concentrate on.

6. As you talk, look directly at one person from time to time. Those sitting around him or her will sense that you are communicating directly with that person and will feel that you are concerned with establishing direct communication with them all.

7. If there is a person in the audience who appears to be hostile and may interrupt you, merely avoid eye contact. By looking directly at him, you will cue in that person, giving him the opportunity to speak. Just ignore him. Look at people you feel are supportive.

Voice projection. Be sure that you always can be heard easily by everyone in the room. On the other hand, don't shout or strain. Try to vary your voice volume. Saying something *softly* can emphasize a point as well as saying it loudly.

Voice inflection. No one wants to listen to a monotone. Vary your pitch and inflection for interest and emphasis. This will add color and energy to your voice and make people want to listen to you. Generally keep the pitch of your voice low: It's easier to hear and carries more authority.

Timing. Like inflection and projection of the voice, the key here is variety. If you change and alter your speaking rate, the audience won't get bored. On the other hand, don't go too slowly or too fast. (Speaking too fast is a common error made by beginning speakers.) Also, learn to use the *pause* effectively. When a speaker goes silent, it is an instant attention-getter. Skillfully placed pauses also allow the audience necessary breathers and opportunities for the information you just gave them to sink in.

Avoid distracting mannerisms. Don't play with the chalk or the pointer, twirl your hair, clench your fists, wring your hands, or stomp your feet. All divert attention from what you are saying to what you are doing. Of course, the "ums," "ohs," and "you knows" in your delivery fall into the same category.

Delivery skills are best when they are *not* observed. Instead, they should enhance and reinforce your words.

Step 10: Final Preparations

At this point you should be well prepared for the actual presentation, and only a few important things remain to be done.

1. Prepare a final detailed outline of your talk two or three days before the actual presentation.

2. Gather all of your materials-visuals-equipment and put them in the correct order of delivery.

3. Have everything ready to go two days before the presentation. On the day before *do nothing at all* about your presentation. This is your "blank day." Try not to even think about it. When you go to bed the night before, briefly review your notes.

4. Eat well and get a good night's sleep the day before your talk. Your body will need the additional energy. (*Note:* Seasoned speakers have learned not to eat sweets right before a talk. It blocks your enunciation.)

5. On the day of the presentation, arrive early enough to set up and *test* any equipment that you will be using. If possible, find the time for one last run-through in the room before people arrive.

6. About an hour or so before you leave for the room, go over your final outline. If it is long, condense it to just one or two notecards consisting of only key words or phrases in the order of presentation. If you have prepared properly, you should need only very brief notes. (Whatever you do, don't write your entire presentation word for word. If you do you will either have a tendency to memorize it, in which case your delivery will sound canned or, if you take it up to the rostrum with you, you will tend to *read* it, which is equally deadly.)

Establishing Audience Rapport

In trying to understand why some people are more successful than others at giving formal presentations, I tried to "crawl into the heads" of a few of the most successful. I learned that each speaker/presentor goes through a series of phases when standing before an audience. Knowing these stages should help you be mentally prepared.

Stage 1: The Big I. The speaker is nervous and preoccupied with herself: "How am I doing?" "What do they think of me?" "Do they like my new suit?" "Is my slip showing?" Dr. Gregory Kunesh, Professor of Speech Communication at the University of Oklahoma, labels this stage "The Big I." If it lasts more than four or five minutes, the speaker experiences an even higher degree of anxiety. If the speaker stays in this stage throughout, she will probably not be successful because the initial nervousness and over-concern for self becomes destructive and prevents the speaker from moving into Stages 2 and 3. The sooner you can move out of this stage, the better off you will be.

Stage 2: Into the Subject. Only by getting involved in the subject matter of the presentation can the speaker forget the Big I. The speakers who seem to really believe what they are saying, who get excited about their subject, are usually the most impressive. If you have really done your homework and are convinced that what you have to say is important, you will find it easier to become involved in your subject. If you can do that, you will soon begin to forget about being nervous. (One way to reach Stage 2 quickly is to cover something that you are particularly interested in near the beginning of your talk.)

However, giving a presentation is more than just beating your own drum about a subject that interests you. If you stay in Stage 2, you run the risk of letting the content of your message run away with you. You lose control of it — and you lose your audience. It is important to move to Stage 3.

Stage 3: Into the Audience. This is the important stage, and this is where you want to go psychologically. At this stage, you genuinely begin to concentrate on your audience. You forget about the Big I, and you capture the audience because you are gearing your message to them.

When you last listened to a good speaker, did she seem to be giving a "canned talk," or did it seem spontaneous — designed on the spot for that particular audience? Chances are that it was not spontaneous, but that the speaker, by concentrating on the audience, was able to adapt her prepared remarks to the needs of that particular audience. How was this done?

The good speaker is amazingly sensitive to an audience's non-verbal cues. When an audience is small and lights are up, the speaker watches facial expressions and body posture and movement for signs of approval, interest, disapproval, boredom, and the like. But even when the audience is larger or when (as in a theater) the lights are out, the good speaker, like the trained actor, receives feedback. The audience tells the speaker where she needs to quicken her pace, tighten or eliminate material that's running too long, where she needs to draw something out, and when she's losing attention. By raising or lowering her voice or pausing for effect, making a gesture or changing position or even abruptly switching from one subtopic to another, she can regain its attention. The speaker can ask the audience a question, introduce an amusing anecdote that she was originally planning to save for later, ask someone in the audience to come up and assist — anything to change the pace, introduce a surprise, or increase rapport. (Note that none of these things is really possible if the speaker is still in Stage 2, or if she lost her audience at the very beginning.)

During a presentation, the rapport you establish with your audience is like a tonic. You begin to make subtle adjustments in your tone, body movements, and choice of words. The self is forgotten. This can be — and often is — totally unconscious at the time you're doing it. Only later can you look back and recall what was happening and why you had forgotten your nervousness and felt good about what you were doing. The process is also cyclical — the better you feel about what you're doing, the better the audience will feel, and the more encouragement you will get.

The secret, then, if there is one to truly great professional speaking, is first, the speaker has an important message; second, the speaker really believes in the message; and third, the speaker adjusts the presentation to each particular audience.

Step #9
Take Risks Decisively

by Kathryn Wakefield

W hen was the last time you took yourself on a tour of your deepest, dearest professional dreams? Picture yourself in the following settings. How are you feeling?

- Your superior agreeing to an unscheduled raise
- Your lover noticing a new excitement about you — new love
- Your coworkers listening and agreeing to your idea
- Retirement funds waiting

Can you see yourself in these situations? And if not, what's holding you back?

What's probably holding you back is the same thing preventing others from exercising their right to dream in real life. Life is a risky business, and in every situation mentioned above there is an element of risk involved.

Any time you embark on something new, something perceived as a departure from the ways of conventional wisdom, you are taking a risk. And taking risks means accepting the possibility of failure. YOU MIGHT FAIL. YOU MIGHT BLOW IT. And no one likes that possibility or is comfortable with that notion. Our natural response, therefore, is to avoid risk, to shun the big chances, and to stay with what we already know.

That's where most people spend their lives — in the safe, predictable world of the Known, never realizing that the Unknown has surprises in store for them, surprises that are hard to glimpse from the armchair comfort of the everyday Known.

On the other hand, people who become comfortable with taking informed, analyzed risks in a career can make profound differences in the quality of their lives.

Taking risks is an inescapable part of modern life. Some people accept risk with ease, taking professional chances too frequently and with such seeming effortlessness they don't even view them as risks. Other people find themselves stuck in unsatisfactory jobs, relationships or situations because they feel trapped, unable to take the calculated changes that could offer them more challenging, productive lives.

Webster's Dictionary defines risk as "the chance of injury, damage, or loss; dangerous chance; hazard . . ." Defining risk in a contemporary business sense is difficult, if not impossible. But here are some common illustrations of risk-taking in the professional world:

Working up the nerve to ask for a raise or a promotion . . . confronting an uncooperative worker . . . requesting extra time off . . . leaving a "secure" job to work with a young, untried company . . . changing careers . . . working independently within your company on a new project . . . leaving a salaried position to become a freelancer . . . ambitiously starting a business of your own . . . all professionals are familiar with these risks.

Whether personal or professional, risks always involve changes and the frightening prospect of facing the Unknown. You are moving away from familiar things — what you have and are comfortable with — into the shadowy realm of the uncertain, toward something which may or may not be better. Risk is always a roll of the dice.

One interesting difference between men and women in the professional arena is their approach to taking risks. Consistent with my experience, and from opinion sampling at my seminars, I've found that male professionals tend to focus on the gains to be made if the risk develops according to plan. This may be due to continued male dominance in positions of authority in the business world. A female professional in the same situation is more likely to concentrate on losses, on what happens if the risk doesn't pan out. Women are less inclined to take risks, partly because we have a shallower reservoir of successful experiences professionally. The extent of our knowledge and savvy is simply more limited and begins when we're young.

For instance, Tommy tries out for the football team. He focuses on making the squad — gaining status with his peers, teachers, family and the prettiest girls in school. Sally tries out to be a cheerleader. She tends to look at the possible negative.consequences of failure — losing self-esteem, being labeled uncoordinated, ugly and unpopular by boys and girls alike.

Taking risks — the big, world-changing kind — is not fun, and this chapter won't attempt to make you think otherwise. What this chapter will do is acquaint you with tips and techniques on professional risk-taking that will help make doing so easier. And the easier the idea of taking risks becomes, the more risks you will find yourself taking. Eventually, you may be taking risks without even recalling how terrifying they used to be. If that sounds improbable, think back to your earlier years . . .

What were some of the pivotal life events that scared you out of your wits at the time, but you went ahead with anyway? Learning to ride a bike or to swim? Trying to break into a new circle of friends? The first time you made a presentation in front of many people? Driving a car for the first time? Making that all-important first date? Those were risks. You knew it then and you know it now. But you followed through with them just the same. And now as a professional, there's no reason to stop taking those risks. There's more at stake. There's more to gain.

This chapter is a ten-step method to plan and execute professional risks to your advantage. It's a way to methodically and categorically chart how to understand and plan risk-taking and how to use taking risks as a springboard to your loftiest ambitions. But a ten-point outline isn't the real key to this chapter. The real magic in making this chapter work is in writing it all down — articulating the situation on paper.

Have you ever kept a journal or a diary, or used the technique of writing lists of pros and cons when considering a new situation? Have you ever written your goals on paper? If so, you may have discovered the incredibly positive things that can happen when you express your thoughts in writing.

Lee Iacocca, the renowned chairman of Chrysler Corporation, is one who understands the transforming process of writing things down. He writes about it in his autobiography: "The discipline of writing something down is the first step toward making it happen."

In *A Passion for Excellence,* Scandinavian Air Systems' President Jan Carlson reveals one of the excellence principles he used to accomplish a major corporate turnaround in just three years. He said, "We don't seek to be one thousand percent better at any one thing. We seek to be one percent better at one thousand things."

It's good advice. Seeing your ideas, particularly your fears and apprehensions, written in front of you helps you address your concerns with appropriate distance. Somehow, the magnitude of a professional risk doesn't loom quite so large and overwhelming once you've taken ideas out of your head and written them down. In our contemporary haste, and with the wealth of things to distract us from doing so, most people tend to overlook the power of expressing their hopes and aspirations on paper. They don't believe that the mechanical process of committing an idea to paper could possibly have the power — the outright magic — of enabling it to become a reality. That so many professionals do write their ideas down (and later succeed beyond their most extravagant dreams) is a testament to how writing it down really does make the difference.

In my twelve years as a career consultant, I have found that writing techniques have eased my clients' fears, and aided in their career transitions. It can do the same for you. Here's how to start: get out paper and pencil, or pen and typewriter, quill and parchment, whatever . . . and start with Step One.

Step One: What Is It You Want?

Let's say you're considering a major professional risk. Before you're consumed with the pipe dreams an increase in salary or change in position successful development of the risk would bring, look at the first issue when considering a risk: Why are you doing it? What do you hope to gain as a result of your efforts? The more clearly you define your objective for the risk at the outset, the more you can focus your energy. It's easier when you are taking the risks for positive reasons, say to find a position which suits your talents better. That's a move *toward* something.

In the real world, however, sometimes you take risks to get away from a boring, confining or otherwise unsatisfactory situation. That means your objective is escape, and that's OK. But it can be more difficult to make such moves. It becomes easier to get bogged down in the semi-comfortable Known than to make that move into the dubious Unknown. In such cases, your thoughts might be something like "Well, this situation isn't the best, but who knows how bad my next move might be?"

There are as many examples of objectives as there are people trying to reach them. Some of the more familiar include:

Leaving a job to start a business with the desire to better use your skills in entrepreneurship, management and sales . . .

Switching from a staff position to sales to potentially increase your income . . .

Requesting a promotion to use more of your talents than the present position gives you . . .

Some people find it easier to evaluate the merits of a risk if it serves more than one purpose — a multiple-objective risk. Moving to a new company not only may provide you with the opportunity to use new skills, but it also gives you the chance to interact in a fresh social environment. The more objectives you have for attempting your risk, the more you can strengthen your motivation. So, on the big, life-changing risks, see how many reasons you can come up with for making the change. One suggestion: write your thoughts as they come to mind. Don't edit them according to how realistic or feasible they are, just get them all down on paper. Part of the magic of written plans is the totally unexpected ideas that appear (remember Mr. Iacocca's approach).

Since your risk has now become a specific goal, with definable features and attributes, we can start using the words "goal" and "risk" interchangeably.

Step Two: Analyze the "Whys"

There are three different ways to analyze your reasons for attempting the risk; each gives you a different perspective on your situation, each strengthens your desire:

a) The payoffs for achieving your goal.

b) The cost of not attempting it.

c) The price of postponement: "What if I don't take this risk now?"

Analyzing the "whys" can be especially useful if significant people in your personal or professional life are discouraging you from taking the risk. One way this is done, in a subtle and seemingly innocuous fashion, is when someone says: "You've got a solid position here and a very promising future. Why in the world would you want to mess up your life by taking a chance like that?" This step helps you offset this kind of thinking with a reply that can short-circuit the power of such discouraging commentary.

A. The Payoffs

Some payoffs are obvious; you'll discover them when you look again at your goals and objectives in Step One. Others are less obvious. Try for a moment to picture how your life will be different if the risk develops. Go ahead, free-associate — if it helps, close your eyes and picture the future. Will you have additional material goods that you don't have now? How will your abilities be stretched, tested and developed? How will you feel about yourself as a result of trying something difficult? How will this change affect other people's view of you, or their relationship with you? Will the change create new opportunities for you?

Life has few guarantees, but here's an "almost-guarantee." As a result of stretching yourself and taking risks, your confidence will grow. It's hard to think of anything better to help your confidence level than to meet challenges and achieve the goals you've selected for yourself.

B. The Consequences of Saying "No"

The basic cost of not even attempting to achieve your risk is obvious. You may find yourself stuck in the same place, even after you've decided that your present situation isn't giving you what you need.

Another cost of not attempting your goal·may be how you'll feel about yourself if you continue to duck the big risks. Seeing yourself as someone who perennially "plays it safe," as a person who avoids challenge, isn't likely to do much for your self-esteem. Call it settling for less. It's like a mountain climber encountering Mount Everest, inching her way torturously toward the top . . . climbing to a level one hundred feet from the summit . . . and then stopping to celebrate right there, secure in the mistaken belief that she's reached the top of the world.

C. The Question of Postponement

Professional opportunities can be random, and sometimes surprisingly frequent. Sometimes you can say "no" to a challenge and basically the same opportunity presents itself in six months or a year. But such instances are generally few and far between. The big challenges in life don't come along very often. For instance, there may not be many chances for you to jump in on the ground floor of a business that grows fast and provides outstanding opportunities for employees with them from the beginning.

Give careful consideration to the consequences of saying "no," and to the question of postponement. Ask yourself seriously if this chance, or another one, is likely to be available at a later time.

Consider the plight of the lean businessman I met at one of my seminars. He was successful but contemplating his future. During the coffee break, he mentioned how he had often avoided taking risks in the past. "I always wanted to be a police officer," he said.

"But I guess I just wasn't comfortable with the risks involved. Now it's probably too late."

"How old are you?" I asked him.

"I'm thirty-two," he said. "I'm not too old to be accepted, but it would still take me three years to pass the Academy examinations and be accepted as a rookie."

"Hmmm ... how old would you be," I asked, "if you went through the Academy examinations and passed?"

"I'd be thirty-five," he said, in a voice he tried to make sound broken.

"And how old will you be in three years if you don't try to get into the Academy?" I asked. He glared at me a moment, as if not quite understanding my question, or its purpose. Then his eyes brightened, his brow arched and he had the expression on his face of someone who realizes the wonders of the perfectly obvious. "Wow!" he said, seemingly awestruck. "You're right — it's the same amount of time either way!"

Some things won't wait for you ... no matter how hard and long you wait for them.

Step Three: Timing and "Stability Zones"

Having looked at what will happen if you don't do it now, let's turn attention to what could happen if you do it now. Ask yourself if now is the right time. Consider two major questions:

First, do you have the stability, security and success in your life to attempt this change and to give it a fair shot?

Take a close look at the present patterns of your life. Are there areas of your life in which you feel secure and successful? It could be your career, your relationships, your avocations or your educational pursuits. It's not important in which area you feel secure, but it is important that you have aspects of your life that give you a sense of well-being and security about yourself and your talents before you take on a major risk.

Most people find they need "stability zones" — the places in their lives where things are under control. These "stability zones" can be a tremendous asset when you are facing the Unknown in other facets of your life. If you don't have any "stability zones" at this time, taking the big, life-changing risk can be somewhat more difficult (though by no means impossible).

Next, ask yourself if you have the time and energy now to give the change an opportunity to develop?

It's a known principle of physics that it takes more time and energy to create something from scratch than it does to sustain it once it's set in motion. Think of the extra hours you put in at the beginning of a new job — hours that weren't necessary after you had "learned the ropes." It's the same with new relationships, new circles of friends or new experiences of any kind.

Generally, we have the time and energy in life to accomplish what we really believe to be important. As my mother used to say, "Kathryn, if he wants to go out with you, he'll call!" However, some changes make tremendous demands on our physical, emotional and intellectual systems. Overloading yourself can lead to self-sabotage. Take a broad, careful look at the demands on your time and energy. Do you have enough of both to let you undertake the big risk?

Step Four: Consequences and Obstacles

Here's where nailing your thoughts down on paper becomes especially valuable:

A. What Could Go Wrong?

This should pose no major challenge for you. You'll probably have no trouble at all coming up with the things that could go wrong. They're the very first things you probably thought of when considering the risk. So go ahead, give Murphy's Law free rein on paper. List every single negative thing that could occur: the new company could go belly up three weeks after you get there ... you won't like the people ... you won't like the city ... you won't meet your quotas ... you won't have the skills to perform well ... the new job will be radically different from what you expected. Be sure and leave space beside each item on your list.

Now for each item on your list, write the answers to two key

questions:
1) What's the probability of this happening?
2) How serious will it be if it does happen?

This is where research into the situation really pays off. But even with appropriate research, you're still making educated guesses.

Perhaps you could use a three-column approach, such as the one diagrammed below. In column one, consider what could go wrong. In column two, ask how probable a disaster could be. In column three, document how serious things could become if the worst that could happen ... happens. Develop a set of numbers or responses that work for you.

Part of a simple list might look like this:

WHAT COULD GO WRONG	CHANCES OR PROBABILITY	HOW SERIOUS IF IT OCCURS
The company might go out of business	Slim and none (very well-financed)	Very
I'll hate the city	Low (past visits were greatly enjoyed)	Somewhat, but could change over time
I'll hate the people I'll be working with	Unlikely (I liked them when we met the first time)	Somewhat, but could change over time

It's also a good idea to buttress your educated guesses with some cold, hard facts. Investigate the company that's considering you. Get an annual report or brokerage reference, if you can, to allay any fears of insolvency. Check the business journals, directories, magazines, the Standard & Poor's corporation listings, the Fortune 500 and 1000 listings. Consult anyone you know who works there for the inside story. (More on this in the chapter on "Networking.")

B. The Fear Factor

Some common fears among women are the fears of success, of failure and of disapproval from friends and family. It's part of a problem that has long been an obstacle for women, an obstacle to progress and advancement.

That problem for professional women is the persistent social and cultural *idee fixe*, in which women have been viewed as being in static positions concerning home, hearth, earning power, and livelihood. Historically, women have been portrayed as the nurturers of our society, the ones who support and nourish the powerful — not the ones who strive to be powerful. Despite many societal advances, women are still perceived as the people who value the emotional over the pragmatic, feelings ahead of results.

Women have a fear of success, but it's not because of any reluctance on our part as women to do the hard work and make the commitment necessary. It's because of social dictates that we've internalized, dictates that aren't that easy to rid ourselves of.

Women are being challenged to make their own decisions. Each is asking herself whether she should have a child, and if so, when? Should she wait to nurture a family until she's gained a confident professional footing? Would a divorce enable her to regain her self-esteem and cultivate her talents or would she feel rejection and wish for marriage's security? Should she remain in the same income bracket or get further training and prove her ability for financial independence?

Achieving success can have palpable and negative effects on the stability of personal life, often because of the very tradeoffs in time and attention necessary to achieve that success in the first place.

And even though we don't have the power to choose whether to be a woman or a man, we are able to choose in which ways we want to develop. At age 57 Eleanor Roosevelt looked back on her life to write, "Somewhere along the line of development we discover what we are to become, and make our real decision for which we are responsible. Make that decision primarily for yourself because you can never live anyone else's life. The influence you assert is through what you become yourself."

Even with the prevalence of the fears particular to women, there is still good reason to articulate the fear factor on paper. Write down your fears in your most negative language; spitting them out raw and without polish is an important step in minimizing their effect.

Put them down like it'll all fall apart tomorrow. And be realistic about the possibilities of failure if you undertake the risk and fail. Failure is possible, so the better you prepare yourself for it, mentally and strategically, the better and more equipped you will be to salvage the situation if everything falls through.

As Chinese philospher Lin Yutang said, "True peace of mind comes from accepting the worst. Psychologically, I think, it means a release of energy."

Step Five: Nailing Down the Reasons Why You Can

A natural tendency is to invest undue time and energy in thinking of all the reasons why you can't do it. You can counteract this by adding an "Upbeat" list to your written thoughts listing every reason why you CAN do it. Be creative, and again, don't mentally edit your options before you write. Just write.

A sample list for a person leaving a salaried position to start a business might look like this:

I've demonstrated my ability to set goals with my freelance work.

I've developed excellent relationships with those freelance clients.

Several of those clients want to give me more work.

I've always been a good salesperson, anyway.

I've got enough money saved to get me through a year if business doesn't develop rapidly.

I get good information and give good advice.

I'm in the best physical shape ever.

I like the idea of being in charge of my own destiny for a change.

The challenge of watching my business grow will compensate for the spare time and recreation I'll probably lose.

When writing your list, think of every situation and every success you've had in the past that even remotely relates to the change you're contemplating now. The more reasons you have, the more you solidify your intent to succeed.

Step Six: The Action Plan

A favorite quote of mine about goalsetting is this: "A goal is just a dream until you put a date on it." Likewise, a risk is just a shot in the dark until you shed some light on it. Here is where we shine a light on every facet of your risk. It is time to commit yourself to action by exploring how to resolve every problematic part of the risk — The Action Plan.

We begin with some more free-form brainstorming. Start writing down all the things you can think of that you will need in order to accomplish your goal: the people to see, the books to read, calls to make, skills to develop, information to find and digest, ideas to discuss ... everything, big and small.

Next, consider a good working order for executing your Action Plan steps.

Then devise the master plan for yourself on paper. Use whatever visual format you are comfortable working with. The key aspect of this step is to get you to commit to a date for execution of (or investigation into) each action step.

Part of a hypothetical Action Plan for someone trying to start her own computer software company might look like this:

DATE	ACTION STEP	CHECK ON COMPLETION
7/10	Call Susan Heller for appt.	
7/11	Read article on independent computer software companies in *Working Woman* magazine.	
7/12	Research similar businesses in books at City Library.	
7/13	Call Small Business Administration for appointment.	
7/14	Attend professional meeting of software designers, XYZ Building.	

That expression "plan your work and work your plan" has particular validity when you are taking a risk. Adhere to your dates and steps as closely as possible. If you need to change a date for an action-step, do it consciously and accommodate your master plan accordingly. It's important that you feel in control of your time and efforts. Whenever you fail to execute an action-step with a well-cultivated excuse, the downward spiral of self-sabotage can begin.

Step Seven: Believe!

That's right, plain old positive thinking. If you've reached this plateau in your planning, you've taken a good look at every side of your particular risk, and decided that you can do it. Now is when you need to make that connection between what you *think* you can do, and what you *know* you can do. Tug McGraw, one-time World Series-winning pitcher for the New York Mets and the Philadelphia Phillies, said it plainly: "Ya gotta believe."

The main element in the success of positive thinking — success proven in numerous testimonials from professional people of all kinds — is this: If you believe you can do it, if the belief in the objective is internalized deeply enough, you're more likely to perform the extra work needed to achieve the objective. That's often the difference between the risk working and the risk falling flat. It's a matter of the extra effort: that extra call when you're bone tired, the extra research when you've seen every book in the library, the extra thinking and concentration, that extra burst of enthusiasm. If you don't believe your plan will work, no amount of drawn-out, half-hearted and supposedly meaningful consideration will change your mind — or the situation. If you don't believe, you have already planted the seed of doubt that will eventually strangle the dream — and the risk — before it ever takes root.

Step Eight: Practice and Preparation in a Low-Risk Environment

Some might call this step "stating the obvious," but it's the obvious that's all too often overlooked.

Generally, no matter what risk you're attempting, some or all of the action steps require new behavior, a need to do things you haven't done before or haven't done well. Honing those skills and behaviors before you need them aids you in feeling more secure and effective when the crunch is on.

Strategies for learning new behaviors in a low-risk environment can include taking the right classes and workshops. A seminar on assertiveness training would enable you to practice handling those changes you anticipate will be consequences of accepting risk: conflict, rude or otherwise insubordinate behavior, rejection of co-worker requests, negotiating a raise or better working conditions.

Or consider role-play situations of your own. Ask a friend to play any one of a variety of roles: your prospective employer, your current employer, a personnel director, etc. Describe the person your friend will play, and tell your friend how you think that person will react. Ask your friend for reactions. If she doesn't believe what you're telling her, ask her why. Not enough eye contact? Too much smiling? Your tone of voice? Practice it until your behavior seems sincere and until you're satisfied with the way you communicate. (More on this in the chapter on "Self-Presentation.")

Sounds like a lot of work, and it is. But the people who do this extra groundwork are the ones whose risks are most likely to succeed. It used to be thought in conventional psychology that you had to change your attitude before you could change your behavior. But that idea has been put into severe question by behavioral and cognitive psychologists. Many now believe that the best way to change behavior is to start with the behavior — first change that and then the attitude will follow.

Envision it. You're in a restaurant with a client, or the object of your affections. The main course arrives, but it's cooler than you would prefer. You take the low-pressure risk of asking your waiter to heat the meal. Suppress that twinge of guilt! You know the one, "How could I have the nerve to call that man over to do this for me! What could I be thinking?" Go ahead, ask. It's a risk, but take it. Then next time, risk something more important professionally. This is the vital incremental nature of venturing risk, that "upping the ante" that has the important effect of making risk-taking both refreshing and challenging.

Step Nine: Support Systems and Reinforcement Techniques

Your plan is in action and you believe you can accomplish the goal. The internal foundation has been laid: you believe you can do it and you've taken the necessary steps to achieve it. Still, there are some times you could use extra jolts of energy and enthusiasm to keep you going, to keep you on track.

Support from your peers can be invaluable in several ways. If you know people who have attempted a similar risk, they may be willing to serve as a resource for you — especially during the rough times when things aren't progressing smoothly. Someone who's been through a similar experience can be a solid source of information, counseling, and empathy.

Even people who haven't exactly "been there" can be of great help if they're positive and share your belief in achieving your goal. They can provide different ways of looking at the situation, give you the benefit of their knowledge in other risky life situations and convey encouragement.

People who can provide practical and emotional support are as precious as jewels; treasure them. Avail yourself of their counsel and experience. And needless to say, try to provide the same kind of solid, unflinching support for them when they need it.

As Isaac Newton said, "If I have seen further, it is because I have stood on the shoulders of giants."

Motivational books and tapes are a fountain of supportive information. Many professionals have found useful such books as *Think and Grow Rich* by Napoleon Hill, *Success Through A Positive Mental Attitude* by Hill and W. Clement Stone, *Your Erroneous Zones* by Dr. Wayne Dyer, *Real World 101* by James Calano and Jeff Salzman, and books by Dr. Norman Vincent Peale and Dr. Robert Schuller. The libraries and bookstores bulge with books designed to inspire people in situations like yours.

Another aid is inside your own head. The technique of visualization is also very important in developing a self-support system.

Find a place where you can be quiet and alone for a few minutes. Then follow these four simple steps:

1) Close your eyes and think about the risk you want to take.

2) Create a mental picture of the risk situation exactly as you would like it to happen. Think in the present tense as if it is already happening that way.

3) See yourself in the situation, going through the motions that lead you to take the risk and succeed. Fill in as many details in the scenario as possible.

4) Focus on your mental picture often, both in quiet periods when you are alone and also casually throughout the day.

These visualization steps will help your mind integrate the positive attitudes necessary to make your visions a reality. Believe you can do it. Enjoy the energy that comes from imagining favorable completion of this project or focus mentally on your past successes. Some people make lists of their former triumphs and post them prominently in their homes. It's a good visual reminder of why you *can* do it.

If you find that rewarding yourself for taking Action Plan steps makes you feel good, do it. A reward could be anything meaningful to you ... fresh flowers ... taking a close friend to dinner ... a mini-vacation ... buying something absolutely frivolous.

"Get serious," you might think. "Do I, a rational adult, really need to reward myself for doing something to get ahead professionally, something to help me accomplish my goal?" No, you don't have to. But if you do, it doesn't make you any less rational, responsible or adult. It merely invests your adventure in risk-taking with something vital to its success: FUN.

Step Ten: Savoring the Little Wins

The risk you are attempting almost certainly falls into one of two categories. Category-one risk is the kind that requires changing your regular behavior, i.e., how you currently handle relationships, conflict, criticism or negotiating on a daily basis. Category-two risk is the less-frequent risk: changing jobs, leaving or beginning a relationship or starting your own business. Each category has its own pitfalls in terms of how you would view the effectiveness of your efforts.

Category-one risktaking requires close monitoring of your behavior for a period of time. When you're learning something new and different, your new behavior can be surprisingly orderly if the concentration is there. I'll use the example of learning to manage conflict effectively. After practicing in a low risk environment, you may handle conflict effectively 25 percent of the time the first week. The second week, you are effective 50 percent of the time. The second month, you handle conflict situations well 75 percent of the time. (Incidentally, these are arbitrary figures used to illustrate the concept, not firm directional guidelines.)

By about the third month, you're likely to be handling conflict effectively about 85 to 90 percent of the time. But if you're like most people, you're probably using your own "selective-attention device," the little psychological mechanism that prompts you to pay more attention to the times you fouled up or reverted to old behavior than to the times when you were most effective.

To counter that mechanism, use a visual recording technique, or even a chart or an appointment book. Charting yourself and your development visually gives you an accurate record of your progress. One method: give yourself a plus (+) every time you implemented your new behavior effectively, an X every time you didn't handle the situation well. This fast and simple charting technique is invaluable, especially if your behavior has slipped and you feel discouraged. Benjamin Franklin, a true American renaissance man, reports in his autobiography how he employed a variation of this technique to help him overcome his personal vices.

In category-two risks (the real life-changers), you may need a different form of recordkeeping to accommodate the wider time scale. With changes of this degree, it can be a long time before you see the changes — or the payoff. Keep careful track of what you have done to get closer to your goal. When it seems as though your efforts will never bear fruit, get out the records. Focus your attention on how much you've done, rather than how much you have to do.

No matter what the risk is you're taking, keeping records of the effort is valuable. It will help you keep on target when you get down and help you savor those little wins . . . the ones that lead to the big victories.

Getting Started

How about starting right now? After all, you've completed the chapter, and the techniques presented here are presumably still fresh in your mind. This is when you can begin your probability of disaster list, your "Upbeat" list and your Action Plan. The faster you write them, the faster you'll be able to use them. And the sooner you'll find yourself taking the risks that matter, personally and professionally.

Taking risks. The words together have an ominous ring, somehow calamitous and deadly. But taking risks need not be a blind plunge into the abyss, or a wild, ill-considered lurch from one professional opportunity to another. When carefully and dutifully considered, taking those major, life-changing risks can be the catalyst for a life of great excitement and reward.

Step #10

Get (or Advance) Your College Degree Without Classes

by Adele Greenfield

Besides your natural and cultivated talents, a college degree is perhaps the most prized and valuable possession you can own, telling the professional world as it does that you have paid your proverbial dues. No matter if you're a graduate of Yale or Concordia, Princeton or Rensselaer Polytechnic Institute, a degree is that indispensable document that confirms your experience in and understanding of a discipline in the intense, and often unforgiving, atmosphere of a collegiate environment. For most professionals, a degree signals their formal entry into the real working world.

Those are the socially accepted facts about the worth of a college diploma, facts that reflect society's intangible affinity for credentials and achievement. Those are the abstracts of getting a diploma. The cold, hard benefits of a college diploma really make a difference on the bottom line. Recent studies have shown that the average college graduate will earn 49 percent more over a lifetime than the average high school graduate — almost half again as much.

155

Clearly, such statistics speak volumes about the value of a college diploma. Put simply, *it pays.*

Yet if you're like most working people involved in the day-to-day experience of working a full-time job, trying to keep your head level with the water (much less above it), you probably think you can't afford to take that valuable time off to pursue a first or second degree, or even to complete work previously started toward a degree.

Well, take comfort in knowing that you don't have to.

The changing face of American education has made it possible to get that degree at your own place, at your own pace, in accordance with your schedule, your syllabus and your personal situation. The external degree has arrived.

In response to the unprecedented change in American life-styles — a change evidenced by emergence of two-income families and single-parent homes, changes such as the assimilation of new veterans, an increase of women entering the workforce and a basic shift in the composition of the population — the external degree, a new approach to college education, was born.

External degrees are legitimate, wholly reputable degrees recognized by all the proper educational authorities, and accredited by the Council on Post-Secondary Education, the official accreditation agency of the U.S. Department of Education. Contrary to popular suspicion, external degrees aren't the dubious, "Learn-in-your-spare-time" credentials hawked on matchbook covers. External degrees are college degrees which can be earned like all college degrees — after demonstration of proficiency in your field. The only functional difference between an external degree and a regular degree is the method by which the external degree is earned. It requires no less work or sacrifice, no less discipline and commitment than with a regular degree. And the rewards are no less satisfying.

There are three main approaches to achieving an external degree, three methods that seek to balance your life as a professional seeking more education with your life as a card-carrying member of the working world. Any or all is bound to be compatible with your lifestyle.

External degrees may be achieved through:
  • Independent study — those courses relying as much on your

initiative and desire as anything else. Independent study courses may be taken at a university or other center of higher learning. While conducted on a consistent schedule like other university courses, independent study courses encourage a student's independence in course work and approach to study, and are therefore ideal for businesspeople, mothers and other people with full-time jobs.

• Experiential learning — Documenting your own life experience in the work arena is also acceptable for work toward an external degree. There's no law that says everything you know from your journeys in life can't be verified by a diploma. The School of Hard Knocks has as many graduates as any college in the country. Your knowledge counts for something, however you come by it.

• Proficiency examinations — These formally confirm one's knowledge of a subject previously learned in an academic setting. This is the alternate route to take when, for example, you started college but could not complete your courses. Proficiency exams are an established way of determining your abilities now, and assessing what's needed in additional education to complete your degree program.

These are the means to an end, the end of getting that diploma you've been thinking about for so long before the object of your affection came into your life . . . before you landed that big position . . . before the kids came and motherhood began to slow you down and hogtie your ambitions. Even with those responsibilities, your pursuit of an external degree can set you free, freer than you maybe thought an academic pursuit could be.

Even though the diploma you earn looks like any other, this is a vastly different educational "delivery system." In an external degree program, you are more in control of your time, and your finances. For example, you can transfer credit for courses you take from other accredited colleges into your program. Let's suppose you have a year of college credit and several years' experience in business and accounting. You may choose to take four different examinations and submit samples of your work for additional credit. Given this scenario, it's possible to end with the equivalent of three years of college credit, saving you two years of work and a considerable amount of tuition.

In such a program, time can be your slave and not your master. Your final "year" could be anywhere from six months to two years, depending on the methods of study you choose, and the courses you select. You might enroll in, say, three different institutions, study a foreign language and take a training program through your company. This is the beauty of the external degree concept: you are tailoring your own education. External degrees allow for an elective approach to your use of time. Since you avoid needless repetition of courses in fields you already know, or the repetition of "survey courses" required by undergraduates, you save tuition money. It's possible to finish more quickly than if you stuck to the traditional classroom-everyday method.

Before we examine the available opportunities more specifically, let's see how two successful women, composites, earned their college degrees off-campus, off the well-beaten educational track.

Patsy Atkinson's erratic travel schedule made it impossible for her to attend classes at the local university. After hours of research, time spent poring over external programs, Pat finally wrote to over 50 accredited colleges to find the best way to complete course work toward a degree in accounting, using her own practical experience. Only three responded.

She enrolled at one of them, but found that surviving in the corporate world and surviving in the educational arena were two very different things. Then she contacted the External Degree Center in Charlotte, North Carolina. As she explains it: "Dealing with the institutions on my own was a hassle. I thought the center could knock out a lot of the red tape, and I was right. They have a working relationship with the university that the individual student can't possibly establish."

With 64 credit hours on her transcript from her previous collegiate background, Pat needed another 64 hours in order to fulfill the requirement of 128 credit hours. Educators at the center worked with her to plan a comprehensive degree-completion program that dovetailed with her career goals, as well as her particular travel and time constraints. The center staff assisted her in gathering material that demonstrated the knowledge she had acquired on the job — learning on a college level but not formalized by a teacher in the classroom. This material was evaluated by the university, which awarded her 34 credit hours toward her degree. She also took college-sponsored correspondence courses and made several academic contacts while traveling around the country. What happened? Pat earned her accounting degree in less than a year.

Pamela Perera was one year short of her marketing degree when she decided to return to school, though not a school in her native Florida. In her search of different external degree centers, Pamela contacted a center in the Midwest. An advisor there helped her to assess where she stood in terms of fulfilling her educational aspirations, and worked with Pamela in choosing the accredited college which best suited her work experience and her own personal objectives. Together, they developed a degree plan with a time frame that was realistic for Pamela, allowing for her special needs, her own personal clock and not that of the university syllabus. If she couldn't get to the center itself, the center staff could come to her through a special interactive computer software program.

Pamela recalls her first exposure to the program. "I was reluctant because I haven't had that much experience with computers. And the idea of getting credit for punching buttons seemed strange to me. But it's great. It's so simple, anyone can use it as long as they have access to an Apple or IBM personal computer.

"I worked for the Department of Social Services in Miami, so I was able to get credit by demonstrating how I applied the principles of human development and behavior to parts of my job.

"Overall, I discovered that I saved a lot of money that would otherwise have gone to tuition payments," Pamela says. "But not only did I save money, I saved time, too."

Pamela's program proved to be so flexible that she could complete her degree work through correspondence, attend an on-campus class at any accredited institution and simply transfer the credits, or perform some independent study courses. She opted for all three plus she took two of the college-level equivalency examinations.

Having successfully passed her three examinations and a university correspondence course in human relations, Pamela received her degree after a two-hour oral assessment.

* * *

Working women have special needs. Colleges are beginning to respond to those needs by offering off-campus alternatives to traditional classroom education and by granting the same degrees earned by on-campus students. This is perhaps evidenced by the increase in women entering college, women responding to the broadening nature of American education. In 1970, some 1,373,000 women over the age of 22 were enrolled in college. By 1980, that number had climbed to almost 3½ million. Just like their counterparts chained to the classroom, graduates of external degree programs continue their advanced study, going on to attend such prestigious schools as Harvard ... Princeton ... Rutgers.

In the case of experiential learning, or application of the "life experience" provisions, you're dealing with intangibles, even more so than you would in a regular classroom setting. Therefore, don't take these experiences lightly. Do your best to make them articulate and worthy of further notice. Write them down. And be prepared to prove you've got the experience you say you have in the crucible of demonstration.

"You've got to demonstrate that you know what you say you know," says Sandra Bommelje Blume, associate director of the External College Degree Center in Charlotte. "While the colleges don't care how you learned the material, you have to show them through documentation such as certificates, examples of your work, slides, tapes, etc., that you are competent in the field in which you're applying for credit."

Different schools use different criteria for assessing a student's past experience. Procedures to determine this knowledge are being constantly updated and refined by the Council for the Advancement of Experiential Learning (CAEL). About 200 colleges and universities meet yearly to share ideas and exchange information concerning CAEL's policies of credit assessment.

Peggy Wetzell, advisor and portfolio specialist at the Center, says that real experience in a field is an attractive plus to managers and executives.

"Whether preparing for a new job or building a program on what they already have, the option of using experience as a foundation for the rest of their educational planning is appealing to managers and other corporate personnel who need degrees themselves, or who send their employees back to school,'' Wetzell said.

Many of you may already be experts in your field — experts without portfolio, without benefit of sheepskin. There's no reason why you shouldn't receive credit for it. The Center helps its clients prepare portfolios — resumes or other written documentation of experience — to get the most credit possible for their particular life experience situations.

Some documents of your experience may not be readily accessible. If you can't come up with the documents you need for a particular field, Blume advises that you take one of the standard college-level proficiency exams. The most widely-accepted examination programs are the following:

• CLEP (College-Level Examination Program), obtainable from The College Board, CN 6601, Princeton, New Jersey 08541. There are 30 exams in general and specific subject areas. Tests cost $30 each.

• ACT PEP (American College Testing Proficiency Examination Program), P.O. Box 168, Iowa City, Iowa 52243. There are some 50 tests in the ACT PEP program similar to CLEP, but many are in occupational fields such as nursing and education. Cost varies from $40 to $225, and is no doubt subject to change.

• DANTES (Defense Activity for Non-Traditional Education Support), from Educational Testing Service, Princeton, New Jersey 08541. Over 50 exams originally developed for the U.S. military, they are now available to the general public.

• Examinations prepared by the colleges themselves to test knowledge are administered throughout the country, and many colleges will grant credit, even colleges other than the one sponsoring the exam.

These tests are given at a number of colleges and testing centers throughout the country.

Another way to get credit for what you know: nearly all of the collegiate institutions included in this chapter accept non-collegiate training and instructional programs (such as those you may have completed in the military or in your job), provided they have been evaluated and recommended for credit by the American

Council on Education (ACE), the national cooperative organization embracing U.S. colleges and universities. Your company's program may be included.

Once the institution of your choice has established your credits, no matter what their source, you must fulfill the degree requirements. More than likely, you won't be doing all of it through your individual college. But most of the time, you will take courses through a variety of learning media and formats such as learning by mail, television courses or via computer. You'll also probably find yourself taking the sources from a variety of institutions outside the sphere of the university itself, then transferring the credit hours to your degree program back on campus.

Quickly now, let's look at some universities and schools through which you may earn a degree:

Chicago State University, Chicago
Eastern Illinois University, Charleston
Governor State University, University Park
Northeastern Illinois University, Chicago
Western Illinois University, Macomb

Degree: Bachelor of Arts.

Special Requirements: Students must take at least 15 semester hours (can be done by mail) from one or a combination of the five institutions in this system. You can take all the courses required for a major, although it's not required to choose one.

Credit for Experiential Learning: Most equivalency examinations and ACE recommendations accepted. You receive 45 semester hours (sometimes more) for a registered nurse's license. The university evaluates documentation of prior learning experiences for credit. This assessment is a real bargain, because there is no limit on the amount of credit which can be earned.

Courses: Independent study courses.

Thomas A. Edison State College,
New Jersey's State College for Adults
101 W. State Street, CN 545
Trenton, New Jersey 08625
(609) 984-1150

Degrees: Bachelor of Arts, Bachelor of Science in Business Administration, Human Services, Applied Science and Technology. A Bachelor of Science degree in nursing is available for residents of the area only.

Special Requirements: There are no time or credit-hour stipulations under Edison's auspices.

Experiential Learning Credit: Most equivalency examinations. They also have their own program, the Thomas Edison College Examination Program (TECEP). Edison evaluates documentation of prior learning experiences for credit. Nurses with a registered nurse's license may receive up to 60 credit hours. Accepts ACE recommendations.

Courses: Edison has no courses. A student takes courses from other accredited institutions and transfers the credit into the program. They offer 100 TECEPs for credit. Other institutional or standard exams can also be taken along the way.

Note: Lower tuition for New Jersey residents.

The University of the State of New York,
Regents College Degrees
Student Services Office
Cultural Education Center
Room 5D45
Albany, New York 12230
(518) 474-3703
(518) 473-8957 (Nursing)

Degrees: Bachelor of Arts, and Bachelor of Science degrees in Business, Nursing, Nuclear Technology, Computer Software, Computer Technology, and Electronics Technology.

Special Requirements: You don't have to go to Albany to get your degree through the program. However, if you want an assessment of your college-level learning acquired through experience or study outside the classroom, a personal meeting with two faculty members would be necessary. This personalized exam can last a day, and takes place at the Cultural Education Center in Albany.

Experiential Learning Credit: Most equivalency examinations and ACE recommendations are accepted. They also have their own exams, the Regents External Degree Examinations and College Proficiency Examinations. For evaluation of documents, see above.

Courses: There are no courses through the Regents Program. A student takes courses from accredited institutions and transfers the credit. As you go through the program, you can take one of their exams or any of several standardized examinations for credit.

Ohio University, External Student Program
302 Tupper Hall
Athens, Ohio 45701
(614) 594-6569

Degree: Bachelor of General Studies (other traditional degrees are available).

Special Requirements: You must complete 48 quarter hours (25% of the degree work) through Ohio University (via correspondence). There is a 48 credit hour maximum on credit for prior learning assessment. However, any credit gained through this assessment may be applied toward the 25% needed through the university.

Experiential Learning Credit: The institution is selective as to which examinations and equivalency programs it will accept. Instances are resolved on a case-by-case basis. The school has its own exams.

Courses: The institution offers independent study courses by mail. You can receive course credit by examination (an Ohio University exam program with study materials sent to you beforehand).

Empire State College, Center for Distance Learning
Office of Admissions
2 Union Avenue
Saratoga Springs, New York 12866
(518) 587-2100, ext. 302

Degrees: Bachelor of Arts, Bachelor of Science, and Bachelor of Professional Studies degrees are available.

Special Requirements: Continual contact with a faculty member, via telephone or mail. Generally, there is a 16-week time limit to complete a correspondence course, and you may complete up to 16 hours per term. You must take at least 32 semester hours with Empire State — four credits are for the phase during which a degree plan is developed.

Experiential Learning Credit: Most equivalency examinations and recommendations from ACE are accepted. All prior experience acquired out of classroom must be demonstrated by passing an exam, with portfolio evaluations.

Courses: Structured correspondence courses are offered, and 28 hours are required through Empire State, in addition to the four planning hours of credit.

Note: This school is designed for students residing outside New York State, but is also available to residents. State residents will experience greater flexibility in scheduling, and pay a lower tuition. Additional degree options and methods of study are available. There are limits on the amount of experiential credit accepted, depending on the degree program. Independent study opportunities are also available.

Eckerd College, Program for Experienced Learners
P.O. Box 124560
St. Petersburg, Florida 33733
(813) 867-1166

Degrees: Bachelor of Arts, Bachelor of Science.

Special Requirements: In addition to a preliminary course outlining goals and how to develop your portfolio, a minimum of eight Directed Study Courses must be taken through Eckerd by mail. Each course is worth 3.5 semester hours.

Experiential Learning Credit: Many but not all of the equivalency exams are accepted. Both exams and ACE recommendations are determined on a case-by-case basis. The institution evaluates

documentation of prior learning experience for credit.
Courses: Directed Study Courses and self-designed majors.

University of Minnesota's University Without Walls
201 Wesbrook Hall
77 Pleasant Street SE
Minneapolis, Minnesota 55455
(612) 373-3919

Degrees: Bachelor of Arts, Bachelor of Science.
Special Requirements: You need 45 quarter hours through the University of Minnesota. Generally one-third òf those are for the degree planning course, and one-third are for work required at the graduation stage.
Experiential Learning Credit: Most standard equivalency exams and recommendation from ACE are accepted. The institution evaluates documentation for credit.
Courses: Only a required degree planning course may be taken by mail. You can take additional correspondence courses through the University of Minnesota, or any other accredited college.

Indiana University, Division of Extended Study
620 Union Drive
GO25M
Indianapolis, Indiana 46202
(800) 457-4434

Degree: Bachelor of General Studies (no major required).
Special Requirements: 24 semester hours of study are required through the Indiana University system's nine different institutions.
Experiential Learning Credit: Many of the standard equivalency examinations and ACE recommendations are accepted. The institution has its own departmental exams.
Courses: The institution offers independent study correspondence courses.

Other, newer options in undergraduate education include:

International University Consortium for
Telecommunications and Learning
P.O. Box 430
Owings Mills, Maryland 21117
(301) 337-4303

Courses are televised in 16 states and two Canadian provinces. It is possible to complete an entire degree program in this method. But there are readings, written assignments, and in many cases, the student must write the exams. Most students integrate the televised courses with either classroom or external degree courses from their college.

The Consortium serves about two dozen colleges and universities, including Pennsylvania State University, University of Maryland, Temple University, and Iona College. Two Canadian universities are also represented. Each institution has its own tuition rates.

Degrees: Bachelor of Arts, Bachelor of Science, and Bachelor of General Studies. Three broad areas of study are available: technology and management, behavioral and social sciences, and the humanities.

Experiential Learning Credit: Most of the colleges award credit upon demonstration of knowledge through examination or portfolio documentation and ACE recommendations.

The Electronic University
TeleLearning Systems,™ Inc.
505 Beach Street
San Francisco, California 94133
(800) 528-6050

This is a telecommunications system which allows you to use a personal computer to take courses and communicate directly with your instructor through electronic mail. A few courses are available now, and more are being developed. Eventually, it is thought that students will be able to complete course work toward a degree with this innovative program. Several institutions are getting involved. Therefore, costs of the courses may vary, depending on the individual institution.

Mirror, Mirror on the Wall, What's the Best Degree of All?

There is no one "best" degree program for everyone, but there is bound to be one program that best meets your personal, career and financial needs. You can get help by writing to the External College Degree Center, 4108 Park Road #212, Charlotte, North Carolina 28209, or by calling the Center weekdays at (704) 525-1163. The staff can guide you in selecting a college and planning a degree program. Once you're enrolled, the Center can serve as your advocate, providing support services as you complete your studies.

Home study courses are another resource which working women are taking advantage of, thanks to reputable trade and technical schools that provide vocational training, schools that have met accreditation standards of the National Home Study Council (NHSC).

To become accredited, each such school performs an intensive study of its own operations, and submits its findings and other instructional-related material for a thorough review by specialists in a given field. The schools are inspected by an external examining committee, and must supply any other information required by the Accrediting Commission. This process is repeated every five years.

"Around 200 of the Fortune 500 corporations use these courses to train their employees," says NHSC assistant director Michael Lambert. "When I started at NHSC over 10 years ago, only 10 percent of the students were women. Now it's 40 percent." There's other evidence that women are now availing themselves of alternative educational opportunities more than before. In NHSC's "Outstanding Graduates of the Year" for 1984, in which twelve students were chosen to represent the three million Americans now in home study courses, eight women were selected by an independent panel as finalists in the competition.

Founded in 1926 under the cooperative leadership of the Carnegie Corporation and the National Better Business Bureau, the NHSC is recognized by the U.S. Department of Education, and the Council on Post-Secondary Education. The network of NHSC-affiliated schools offers some 1,500 courses by mail and, besides written materials, many courses provide tapes, tools, samples and other equipment.

The mechanics to home study courses is simple. You receive lessons in the mail, complete them and return them to the school, usually in mailers with postage already attached. An instructor critiques your work and sends you additional assignments. In this way, you are developing a personalized student-teacher relationship, albeit not one that's face to face.

You may arrange to take examinations at a testing site such as a local school or library. The average course of study lasts 18 months, but the rare course is available that runs to either extreme: as short as one to two months, or as long as four years. Tuition costs vary widely, too, ranging from no charge to $4,000, and averaging between $700 and $1,000 for a complete program.

Less than 10 percent of the NHSC-affiliated schools offer degree programs, so if you're in the market for one, check carefully. But you can improve your leverage as a professional with correspondence and home study courses. Without the rigors of traditional classroom study, you can learn the fundamentals of hotel management, occupational safety, gemology, engineering design, Montessori instruction, insurance underwriting or travel booking. How about hospital technology? Accounting? Small business management? Yacht design? The opportunities are virtually limitless.

Write to the National Home Study Council at 1601 18th Street N.W., Washington, D.C. 20009, for a free directory of accredited correspondence schools. Contact those that interest you, and take it from there.

Doing Your Homework

You've decided to enroll in either a college or trade school, or to give correspondence school a try. It's time to ask yourself some important questions, to get the best possible handle on which school or course is likely to best serve your needs.

- What's the school's past record for scholastic excellence and student satisfaction?
- Do the promotional materials match the actual services they can realistically deliver?
- Are the staff members competent to address your needs?
- Do you get specific answers to specific questions, or are you now just a victim of the runaround?
- How much will you be paying, and on what timetable? Will your company reimburse you? Does the institution in question have a refund policy?
- How long will the program take to complete?
- Are YOU self-motivated, enough so to work in the relative isolation of home study, correspondence or other off-campus educational formats?
- Do you have, or are you willing to take, the time and personal energy to devote to this and to see it through to the finish?
- What other resources are available from your company, your community?
- Will your friends and family members be cooperative? If you live at home, can you arrange to have the quiet time you'll need?

Don't be afraid to call the schools. If they're not available for you now, they won't be around later, either.

And as in any scholastic effort, be sure to do your homework when you're considering additional education. Investigate the institution thoroughly. Unfortunately, our little rejoinder earlier in this chapter about "dubious credentials" doesn't stop at just offers printed on matchbook covers. Such credentials are often foisted on the public under the guise of honest, legitimate degrees.

Beware the "diploma mills," the small and nebulous pseudo-companies whose business it is to manufacture diplomas by request. Know that these quack-degree shops are "numerous, tough and aggressive," according to an August, 1985 study by the American Council on Education.

It would be comfortable to adopt a benign attitude toward the diploma mills, assuming that only the more unenlightened would even consider using their services. That's generally true, but diploma mills are becoming more and more sophisticated in their methods. The ACE study also noted that there are more than 30 fake accrediting agencies, dummy companies that give diploma mills an aura of legitimacy.

Worse, the taint of the diploma mill spreads even to the solidly established, nontraditional educational programs at reputable universities. The misconception arises in the public mind that "they're all the same," the shoddy, valueless diploma mills and the real, valid programs that give credit for thoroughly documented experiential learning.

Not all unaccredited programs are products of the diploma mills. Some schools offering off-campus, experiential or correspondence programs are licensed by the state, but may not be accredited by either the National Home Study Council, or any of the six regional accrediting associations recognized by the Council on Post-Secondary Education. Check with educational authorities in your area.

Maybe the key to avoiding the diploma mill scam is sticking with the names and institutions you know. The solid ones, the ones with their reputations established over time. Sure, the frauds should be easy to spot, but if not, consult your state's public education department, administrators of your state university's board of regents or your local Better Business Bureau.

And if all else fails, just remember life's all-time common sense fact: you never get something for nothing. Any guarantee of a diploma with the performance of little or no academic work is utterly bogus. Forget it.

Going Back to School. It's maybe one of our society's most loaded phrases, filled as it is with visions of school supplies, reams of paper, a library of books you're responsible for buying, another library of information you're responsible for digesting in a seemingly impossible amount of time. But it doesn't have to be. If you've got the commitment, the willpower and the drive, you can make your own off-campus, on-the-job education reality, a reality consistent with your own pace.

No matter which way you attempt it, it's a decision that will require dedication. But if you're methodical in your search for the best institution, and cautious about the institutions that aren't institutions at all, you'll find life at E.D.U. (External Degree University) can be a rewarding challenge.

Good luck!

For more information, write:

American Council on Education
One Dupont Circle
Washington, D.C. 20036

Step #11

Manage Your Stress and Energy Level

by Bee Epstein

R emember the stereotypical overworked executive staying late at the office, taking work home, finally nursing an ulcer? His family and doctor tell him to relax, but he doesn't listen. Finally, he feels chest pains and ends up in the hospital with a heart attack.

Remember? Well, lately it seems that he is a she. Fifty-four percent of the adult female population is now in the work force. Twenty-one percent of these women are in managerial positions and 55% of all American children have mothers who work outside the home. Studies by the National Heart, Lung and Blood Institute have found heart disease increasing among married working women with children. Smoking, alcohol consumption and drug use among women are on the rise. More and more career-oriented women are experiencing the stressors that were once the man's badge of achievement: long work hours, no time for the family, and self-neglect.

173

WHAT PRICE GLORY

The financial manager is negotiating a
    new loan
I helped him with a strategy
    My son wants to drop out of school
But I come home too late at night
    to spend time with him

The vice president in charge of production
    is not meeting schedules
I helped him plan
    My daughter is living with this guy
        I don't like
But I work on weekends and don't have time
    to talk to her

The lawyer is fighting an antitrust suit
    I helped him write a brief
My spouse is leaving me
    because I am never home
But I don't have the time to go on vacations

The sales force is not meeting forecasts
    I provided new incentives
The doctor says I must take it easy
    But I don't have the time. . .

Natasha Josefowitz (reprinted with permission)

A recent nationwide survey of 40,000 working women found that, contrary to myth, stress is not limited to executives. Women at all levels experience stress. Executive women report that they have highly stressful jobs. However, they are in a position to make decisions, have control and turn stress into productive energy. Women in lower level positions say they have hassles, hectic lives or suffer from "nerves." Surprisingly, they experience more of the stress-related illnesses than do executive women. Many studies indicate that lack of power, inability to control the pace of one's work, repetitious, tedious work and lack of challenge on the job all contribute to stress-related illnesses. These illnesses generally appear in lower-level occupations. No woman is immune from the effects of stress. She must learn to manage it.

What Exactly Is Stress? Stress is a word coined by Dr. Hans Selye to describe a complex series of biochemical changes that occur in the body when the brain or central nervous system perceives a threat to its well-being. The body sets up the alarm response, a primitive response designed to help the organism protect itself. In the distant past, the primitives were affected by episodic stressors such as natural disasters, thunderstorms or encounters with wild animals. The primitive's alarm response, which includes increased adrenalin flow, heart rate, muscular strength and other related physiological adjustments, helped her gather the physical strength to fight or run from the danger. Dr. Walter Canon described this phenomenon found in all animals as the "Fight or Flight" response.

Modern woman also has her share of episodic stressors. However, she rarely fights or runs. Instead, her body adapts. Worry, guilt, long-term time pressures, confronting the problems of being a woman in the business environment, questions about her role in society, running a home and career — they're all stressors. These also cause similar adaptive biochemical changes in the body. Over a period of time the body runs out of adaptive energy, and stress-related illness shows up.

Signals and Symptoms of Excess Stress: Many women don't recognize stress until it gets out of hand, but we do have plenty of warning. The following are some of the common symptoms of stress:

headaches	muscle tension
stiff neck	back pains
digestive problems	appetite change
teeth grinding	tics, nervous habits
colds, minor ills	anxiety
mood swings	depression
irritability	fatigue
isolation	distrust

blaming	crying
sleeplessness	too much sleep
low self-esteem	loss of interest in sex
excessive alcohol use	use of drugs

Most people are able to live with some of these symptoms, but when stress becomes prolonged, it results in serious health breakdown. Research indicates that the following conditions are often the result of excess stress:

heart attacks	high blood pressure
stroke	ulcers
arthritis	kidney disease
cancer	respiratory problems
accidents	

How to Evaluate Stress Levels

Life Change Units: In the late 1960s, Drs. Thomas H. Holmes and Richard H. Rahe published the Social Readjustment Scale, a test that became the standard for measuring stress. This test is widely reproduced in books and articles on stress. It is based on Life Change Units. The test lists 43 events shown to produce stress. These events range from death of a spouse, which earns 100 points, to divorce (73 points), fired at work (47), retirement (45), son or daughter leaving home (29), vacation (13), to minor violations of the law (11). According to the researchers, if a person's total score reaches a certain level, there is increased risk of experiencing a significant health problem in the near future.

I took this test several years ago. According to my score, my stress was at a dangerous level. During the time I was working on my doctoral degree, I went through a divorce, changed employment, my father died, and I had significant financial loss. My score was close to 500. Three hundred was the point at which Holmes and Rahe's research showed that I was subject to a serious illness down the road. That scared me and I began a study of stress and how to control it in my own life. Since then I have been very successful managing stress. Even though I am still subject to the same stressors that bother other working women, I am generally calm, under control and able to handle any situation without undue stress. I am energetic and healthy, and my general attitude and sense of well-being are exceptional.

For several years I have been sharing my experiences and knowledge with others. Those who use the information and coping strategies available to them are able to control excess stress and improve the quality of their lives.

Much of my professional work has been with women. I discovered that my personal experience was commonplace among working women in all professions. We are constantly coping with problems that don't show up as events on the Holmes and Rahe Scale. The conditions of our everyday lives seem to take more of a toll than the occasional dramatic stressful events in life. For example, studying and working on my doctoral degree meant that I had far less time to take care of my family's needs. Trying to meet as many of their needs as I could, or the guilt when I chose to do my work instead, caused me constant conflict. The pressures of scheduling and juggling study, work and family were always with me. Because I was choosing a non-traditional role, I had little emotional support from my family. Add the financial pressures of the cost of graduate school and fewer working hours and you have someone with a strong stress foundation. At that time I was the "E" type woman, which psychologist Harriet Braiker describes as the woman who tries to be Everything to Everybody. The modern woman not only cooks the bacon, she helps bring it home, too. This is the new norm in the U.S. today.

Women are entering the work force in increasing numbers. In 1900, only 20% of the total female population was in the labor force. Most of these women were single and worked out of necessity. In 1984, 54% of the female population was employed outside the home. This has produced dramatic changes in the family and in our value system. The stereotypical American family — with a father who supports his wife and two children — represents only 7% of all U.S. families. More and more single professional women choose to have and raise children alone. Women no longer have clear-cut roles, and this affects men and children also. This underlying stressor is so pervasive that it is considered a normal part of life.

Women have joined the "rat race" that has traditionally been a source of stress for men, but women have additional stressors. They must learn to adapt to the corporate world, work with men in new roles and compete for advancement. Women face discrimination and wage inequities in the workplace. These problems add to the juggling act of balancing home, family and a personal life. Modern woman is "Superwoman." The "Superwoman Syndrome" is synonymous with excess stress. This syndrome is not included on tests that measure Life Change Units. Superwoman's stress is not limited to isolated dramatic events. Her stress is a condition of her lifestyle. This chronic stress must be recognized and evaluated if a woman wants to get an accurate look at her total stress. It is the chronic stress that ultimately wears the woman down.

Stress Test for Working Women

The questions on this test help you evaluate the chronic stressors that are part of being a woman in the work force. Some questions concern your work and others your personal life. Some can be interpreted either or both ways since it is often difficult to separate the effects of work and personal stress. Score yourself on each question: 0 for never true; 1, rarely the case; 2, sometimes. Give yourself 3 if the statement is true about half the time, 4 if it is often the case, and 5 for a statement that is almost always true.

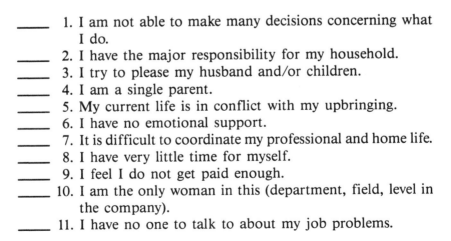

_____ 1. I am not able to make many decisions concerning what I do.

_____ 2. I have the major responsibility for my household.

_____ 3. I try to please my husband and/or children.

_____ 4. I am a single parent.

_____ 5. My current life is in conflict with my upbringing.

_____ 6. I have no emotional support.

_____ 7. It is difficult to coordinate my professional and home life.

_____ 8. I have very little time for myself.

_____ 9. I feel I do not get paid enough.

_____ 10. I am the only woman in this (department, field, level in the company).

_____ 11. I have no one to talk to about my job problems.

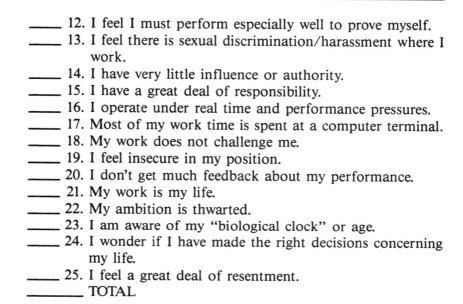

_____ 12. I feel I must perform especially well to prove myself.

_____ 13. I feel there is sexual discrimination/harassment where I work.

_____ 14. I have very little influence or authority.

_____ 15. I have a great deal of responsibility.

_____ 16. I operate under real time and performance pressures.

_____ 17. Most of my work time is spent at a computer terminal.

_____ 18. My work does not challenge me.

_____ 19. I feel insecure in my position.

_____ 20. I don't get much feedback about my performance.

_____ 21. My work is my life.

_____ 22. My ambition is thwarted.

_____ 23. I am aware of my "biological clock" or age.

_____ 24. I wonder if I have made the right decisions concerning my life.

_____ 25. I feel a great deal of resentment.

_____ TOTAL

This is an indicator, not an exact measure, because some people can tolerate a greater number of stressors than others without feeling ill effects. If your score is below 40 you do not have much chronic stress in your life; 40 to 59, you shouldn't have too much concern. If your score is between 60 and 79 you would do well to practice stress management techniques, and if your score is 80 or over, you should make stress reduction a priority.

Effective Coping Strategies: Stress involves a deterioration in physical and mental health. The most immediate and beneficial way to control stress is to take care of the body so it has the strength and energy to withstand the damaging effects of constant physiological adaptation. Shifts in attitudes and expectations also have a considerable effect on stress reduction. Actually, controlling stress comes down to controlling attitudes and behaviors.

Good Nutrition: Several years ago, when I didn't feel very well, I went to my doctor to determine why. I had migraine headaches, several minor physical problems, and also suffered from general lethargy and depression. At that time I had little awareness of the concept of stress. So my doctor decided to treat one of my symptoms and prescribed a drug to improve my frame of mind. Sure enough, I began to feel better.

We have known for years that drugs can affect mental states. Drugs are just substances which we put into our bodies to produce biochemical changes. Doesn't it make sense that anything we put into our bodies can affect us? Almost everyone is aware of how alcohol or caffeine makes them feel, but most people do not know how their bodies are affected by the other things they eat and drink.

"You are what you eat" is an old cliche, but it is so true. A direct relationship exists between what we eat and our sense of well-being.

When people eat the kinds of foods that provide vitamins, minerals and other essential nutrients, bodies work well. When we put things into our bodies that either have no nutritive value or have harmful effects, our bodies do not have the necessary fuel to run effectively. You would not think of running an expensive car on inferior fuel. It would not perform well, and it would wear out more quickly. Are you trying to run your body on inferior fuel? When the body is not fueled well, it must use reserves of vitamins, minerals and other nutrients just to function. The body does not have the extra energy to cope with stress.

A great deal of research has been done on health, stress and food. There is general agreement that the individual who eats well responds less severely to stress. And it is also known that certain substances actually cause stress. The woman under chronic stress can make a significant improvement in her well-being if she consciously controls what she puts into her body.

What to Avoid

1. Alcohol. Most people think alcohol is a relaxer. They sit down after work and have a drink, or they go to "happy hour" at the local lounge to drink with their friends. Actually, alcohol produces reactions in the body that cause additional stress and deplete the body's store of the "stress" vitamins, B and C. It is the sitting down or being with friends that is the genuine stress reducer, not the alcohol. Alcohol temporarily makes you forget your stressors, it doesn't make them go away. That's not to say an occasional drink is wrong. What is wrong is relying on alcohol to unwind.

2. Tobacco. Women's death rate from lung cancer has increased threefold in the last ten years. That's the first, most obvious drawback. Another problem with cigarettes is their interference with the body's ability to absorb and use the vitamins and other nutrients in food. The body needs vitamins and minerals to cope with stress. But smoking also creates social stress. Other people don't like to be around smokers. An eligible bachelor friend said that he refuses to date women who smoke. He can't stand the odors they carry around with them.

3. Caffeine. Caffeine is a stimulant. It triggers the same physiological responses as stress. Excess caffeine intake has been found to play a significant role in some cases of anxiety and depression. The amount of caffeine in three cups of coffee is about all the body should have to tolerate each day.

4. Sugar. Refined sugar has been shown to negatively influence behavior and moods. It also contributes to extra weight since it has a lot of empty calories in a small amount. I'm sure you have heard that sugar gives you quick energy. This is true. However, that energy rush lasts a very short time and because of the influence on insulin production, you will experience the need for another jolt of sugar within a short time. That's how chocoholics are made. One of the worst things you can do when you experience stress on the job is to sit down with a cigarette, a cup of coffee and a doughnut. You'll be down again in half an hour. Instead, try some of the stress reducers we'll discuss later.

5. Salt. Salt causes water retention. Water retention can affect our moods. It also is a primary cause of high blood pressure. Stress causes high blood pressure, too. High blood pressure contributes to heart attacks and strokes. The average American woman gets 20 times more salt per day in her diet than is necessary for health.

6. Fat. Stress causes excess accumulation of cholesterol in blood vessels. This causes atherosclerosis and related heart diseases. Add the cholesterol in saturated and animal fats and you have a problem.

Red meat, especially marbled, is high in fat. Processed lunch meats and most snack chips are incredibly high in fat and salt. Avoid these.

7. Bleached flour. When brown whole wheat is processed and turned into clean white flour, 26 nutrients are discarded in the process. (What is removed is the wheat germ which is then sold in health food stores to put vitamins and minerals back in the diet.) However, the flour is then enriched with four synthetic vitamins. The fiber content needed to keep the digestive system functioning is missing. Remember, stress contributes to problems with digestion.

Eat More of These Healthful Foods

1. Fresh fruits and vegetables. Fruits and vegetables are natural sources of sugar, fiber, carbohydrates, vitamins and minerals. A raw apple can satisfy the body's craving for sugar and also provides fiber and a host of vitamins. It fills you up, is far more satisfying and healthier than a candy bar and doesn't have any harmful ingredients. Stay away from canned fruits and vegetables; many are full of sugar and salt.

2. Whole grains. Again, a wonderful source of fiber, vitamins and minerals. Cereal and breads made from whole grain flour are also more filling than those made with refined flour so you get full on fewer calories. This contributes to weight control.

3. Fish and chicken. These are our healthiest sources of animal protein. They have far less fat and fewer calories than red meat.

More Suggestions for Reducing Stress with Diet

1. Pay close attention to what you are putting in your body, but don't be compulsive. The non-healthful foods in moderation aren't going to damage you permanently. It's okay to have a drink or a candy bar or french fries once in a while.

2. Don't go on a fad or popular weight reduction diet when you are under unusual stress. You will just get irritable, and may deprive yourself of needed nutrients. You can lose weight by changing your eating habits to those outlined here. The personnel manager for a major manufacturing company said, "Since I have

changed my eating habits, I find that I am able to eat more and yet I am losing my unwanted pounds."

3. Stay away from convenience and processed fast foods. They are full of unknown ingredients that contribute to the physiological stress response.

4. Apply this general rule of thumb: If it grows it is probably okay to eat. If it has been manufactured in a stainless steel vat and wrapped in cellophane, it probably isn't. Read labels.

Controlling Stress With Mental Relaxation

"The best time to relax is when you don't have time to relax."

This technique can relax you in a matter of minutes. You know that the worry, guilt and "should" thoughts in your mind can produce stress. As a matter of fact much of the stress we feel is a result of our own thoughts. If we can think ourselves into stress, we can think ourselves into relaxation. Thoughts that are relaxed make our muscles relax. Many women say that their tension headaches go away after five to 10 minutes of mental relaxation. Mental relaxation is often called visualization, but it is really what we commonly call daydreaming. When our minds wander to wonderful places and thoughts, we feel guilty because we're not concentrating on the issues at hand. But the daydream or mental relaxation gives us a chance to bring body processes back to normal.

Try this exercise: Shut your eyes. Take a deep, slow breath. As you breathe in, feel the tension in your body. As you breathe out, imagine this tension flowing down from the top of your head through your shoulders, down your arms and out your fingertips. Take another deep breath, and as you let this breath out, imagine tension flowing down your torso, through your legs and out the tips of your toes. Take several breaths until your body feels completely relaxed. Now let your mind go back to a time and place in which you felt totally relaxed. It might have been a childhood experience, a vacation, time shared with a special person. While you continue your deep breathing, eyes still closed, relive that experience. Transport yourself to that time and place. See yourself in your imagination doing what you did then. Breathe that air, smell those smells, see those colors.

Nicole Schapiro, nationally known speaker and consultant who travels more than 200 days a year, says she often relaxes in busy airports by transporting herself to nature and lush green hills. Another friend replays a fantastic tennis game. I lay by the side of a swimming pool, hear the splash of the swimmers and feel the warm sun on my body. Choose your own special place. Go there whenever you feel tense, anxious or need to unwind. Practice until you have perfected this technique. You will find yourself far more refreshed and rejuvenated than when you try to relax with a drink.

Exercise Away Tension

Bodies have joints and muscles because bodies were meant to move. People were not designed to function comfortably in cubicles called rooms or offices, and get from place to place in rolling cubicles called cars. Yet that is how we live. We are trying to adapt to civilization, and adaptation is a stressor. To get rid of some of our stress, we must use our bodies for the things they were designed to do. People who exercise regularly are healthier and live longer than those who are sedentary. Unfortunately, the working woman is often in a position that keeps her inactive. Most office equipment that women use causes muscle strain that adds to the stressors already present in the working environment.

Ideally, to get into good physical condition a person should exercise actively at least three times a week. This exercise should be of the aerobic type; that is, it should make your heart beat at 75% to 80% capacity. This should continue for 12 minutes. According to exercise expert Covert Bailey, the elevated heart rate changes metabolism rates and is instrumental in general fitness and weight control. Not everyone is striving for top physical fitness. We're looking at stress reduction, so other programs might be better for you. Dance classes such as "Jazzercise" are popular with working women. These classes are scheduled in the early evening, and for the really dedicated, sometimes at 6 a.m. If you can't quite manage that, you can do other things to energize yourself and relieve your minor aches and tensions. For example:

1. Jump on a trampoline. I have a mini-trampoline in my bedroom. A doctor friend has one in her office. I like it because it is the ideal lazy person's exerciser. When I am too lazy to change my clothes and go to the club to play tennis or work out in the exercise room, I jump on the trampoline while I watch the evening news. So while I get stressed over world conditions, I relieve that stress by jumping it off.

2. Walking is excellent exercise. If you walk at a brisk rate for 30 minutes a day, you will be getting an adequate amount of exercise. The time spent walking to the coffee pot does not count. The walking should be done outdoors in comfortable shoes.

3. Do stretching exercises at your desk. You will feel better. Neck rolls regularly will relieve neck tension. If other people see you exercising and think you're crazy, that's okay. Part of your stress probably comes from trying to live up to other people's expectations. You can get rid of that stressor at the same time.

Exercise is so beneficial because it triggers the parasympathetic nervous system which acts to normalize body processes. When a person exercises, she uses her muscles the way nature intended. This contributes to normal circulation and relief of tension. The best reason for regular exercise is that it makes you feel better. Sue works out in the exercise room at the athletic club. She grimaces and complains during her whole routine. When I asked her why she does something she doesn't like, she said, "I always feel so good afterward. I have more energy and my disposition improves." Recent research suggests that exercise also has a biochemical effect on the brain, producing creativity and clarity of thought. Some of my best thoughts come on the tennis court. Many of my professional friends tell me they have their best ideas in conjunction with exercise. Exercise time is not a luxury for the working woman . . . it is a necessity.

Manage Time to Manage Stress

Lack of time is a major stressor for most people. The working woman with a family has the greatest problem because she must put in her regular work week and also keep up with her other full-time job — that of a homemaker. Research shows that the working woman puts in an average of four hours per day after her paying job is over. The working man averages 30 minutes per day in household tasks.

My client, Jennifer, said, "After my workday I have to shop for the family or pick up the baby from the sitter's house. Then I have to fix dinner. My husband helps, which I appreciate, but I still have the overall responsibility. I seem to be tense and irritable much of the time and have very little energy. My personal life isn't satisfying; things aren't working out too well." I asked Jennifer what would help reduce her stress and she said, "More hours in the day." Actually, Jennifer doesn't need more hours, she needs to manage the ones she has. Good time management techniques are also stress reduction techniques.

Time management involves making out a written schedule and ordering priorities. The working woman must schedule stress reduction time for herself because too much stress shows up in health breakdowns. Health is a number one priority. Good health is not an accident. It is a result of self-care. The working woman must make self-care integral to her calendar and then keep her appointments with herself. As the administrative details of life call of our attention, it becomes too easy "not to have time" to exercise; take a long, hot bath; take a walk on the beach. But if these things are on the calendar and take top priority, they will get done.

The successful women I work with know that their physical and mental health is a priority. Jessica Fullmer, a very successful colleague, told me that she goes to her health club three mornings a week at 6, works out for 45 minutes, then showers and dresses in a leisurely way and begins her work day at 8. One of my clients, a high-level executive for a major manufacturing company, said that she uses half her lunch hour to take a vigorous walk. Another said she schedules an hour before dinner to completely unwind (without a drink) as a good way to make the transition between work and home. Every woman can come up with a creative way to schedule self-care time. I know that many women feel guilty when they begin taking time for themselves. They feel they are neglecting their families. I do know that those who persist in making their own time get over the guilt. Their dispositions and energy improve and their families ultimately reap the benefits.

Recognize Your Value as a Human Being

In a male-dominated society, it is very hard for many women to feel truly "equal." Yes, I know we have been given "equality" under the law, but in reality we do not get equal pay or opportunity. The outward struggle for equality in the business world is one stress, and often our emotional acceptance of our lesser value adds to it. Janet, a bank vice-president, said to me, "I am the highest-ranking woman in this bank. There are three levels above me, and I know I'll never get any higher than I am. The men at my level have reasonable expectations of promotion. My expectations are nil." When I talked to her, Janet was close to exhaustion. Reorganization was occurring at the bank and some positions were unfilled. Somehow, Janet was the person usually staying late. When I asked her why she overextended herself so much, she said, "There are so many loose ends. Someone has to take care of them!" Janet's behavior — as a troubleshooter and as someone trying to take on the burden of extra responsibilities — suggested that she saw little value in herself, but great value in what she did for others. She was reinforcing her stressors.

In addition to her workload, Janet had teen-age children and spent her weekends on family needs. I asked Janet when she was going to take care of herself. "After I get everything else taken care of," she said. "It won't be too much longer." Janet put herself in last place and suffered from it physically. Her migraines were consistent. Since Janet put herself in last place, so did everyone else. When she couldn't cope any longer, she was ready to acknowledge that she deserved help.

I told Janet that she had to see herself as important as everyone else in her life. She had to protect her time and her health. To do this she had to negotiate with others for equitable distribution of the workload at the office. For example, instead of automatically taking on extra responsibilities, Janet might evaluate what had to be done and then talk to her peers at work saying, "Here is a list of OUR additional projects this week. Let's divide them among us."

Janet also had to express her needs to her family and work out time when she came first. "I found that when I did this, my children were relieved. My 'sacrifice' for my children showed up in resentment. I was not terribly pleasant and the children felt guilty for 'taking advantage' of me. No one was happy. When I began to say 'no' or 'not now' to them, everyone felt better. I was setting limits for them and taking care of my needs. My stress level dropped, I felt physically and emotionally better and this reflected itself in my behavior."

Keep Your "I Love You's" Up-To-Date

I enjoy reading the advice columns in the newspaper. I get a sense of what bothers people. Many problems which Ann Landers or Dear Abby addresses are things that some of us think are ridiculous, but each letter was written by someone stressed enough to need help. Unfortunately, these people didn't have the support of friends — so helpful in reducing stress. Instead they wrote to a friendly stranger.

Sometimes people write to give advice rather than get it. At regular intervals someone writes to tell readers to let people know you love them. A typical comment: "My father died last week. I always meant to let him know how much I appreciated what he did for me, but I never got around to expressing it; now it is too late. Don't let it be too late for you."

A standard male comment goes something like this: "I work hard to provide a comfortable home for them. They have a nice car, clothes, piano lessons, the best of everything. They know I love them; I wouldn't knock myself out like this if I didn't!" Working women are beginning to think and say the same things. Lack of openly-expressed love is a major stressor for all family members. TELL the people you love that you love them. What you spread around comes back to you. Sheila Murray Bethel, top woman sales trainer in the country, travels constantly. Sheila and her husband, Bill, speak to each of their six grown children every week. They use the telephone to keep their "I love you's" up-to-date. Keeping "I love you's" up-to-date brings peace of mind, the opposite of stress.

Most people are very good at expressing themselves when something goes wrong, but they have a much harder time expressing positive feelings. This is especially true for people under stress. They have a tendency to find fault or blame others. It doesn't feel good to be blamed or criticized — or to do the criticizing. Criticism is a stress generator.

Try this technique. It worked for me. Next time you come home exhausted, walk into the house and find several things to criticize — coats all over the dining room table, chores undone, apple cores, empty pop cans and dirty dishes on the floor of the den and the family glued to the TV set — hold back your inclination to rant and rave. Just stop. Take a few deep breaths. As hard as it may seem at this moment, give your family what you need most right now — love and appreciation. You will be setting the stage for harmony in the household, which is what YOU need. Ranting and raving may get the chores reluctantly accomplished, but it will also create stressful feelings.

When you think loving thoughts you will notice that your breathing slows down, your muscles relax and you will be aware of a smile on your face. This is a state of relaxation. When you express your love to others, you will be creating an environment in which everyone's feelings of self-worth and love are enhanced.

Keep your "I love you's" up-to-date for yourself, too. This is especially important for single mothers who get little support from others. I find that pampering myself reduces my stress. I love flowers, so often I will buy a bouquet for myself, because I deserve it. When I have done an especially good job with something, I reward myself. If I have had a trying day, I do something nice to compensate for my difficulties. This way every day ends on a positive note rather than in frustration and stress.

The techniques we have discussed so far can form a foundation for stress reduction. They are various "self-care" techniques. These are the most effective because a woman does have control over herself, her thoughts, her attitudes, responses and general behavior.

She does not have control over others or many circumstances. The emotionally strong, physically healthy person has high self-esteem, confidence and the ability to make appropriate decisions. She is able to effectively cope with things beyond her control. Turning her attention to maintaining her physical and mental health is the woman's first defense against the destructive effects of excess stress.

Dealing With Stressors At Work

So far we have looked at general conditions that cause stress for women. Now let's look at specific workday situations that are among the top causes of stress for women.

Too Much to Do and Not Enough Time: Very few people spend enough time planning and scheduling. I have found that proper planning eliminates many time wasters. Planning projects, scheduling your week and detailed planning of each day will give you control of your time at work. Another excellent technique is to make a list of all your projects and tasks and ask your supervisor to help you plan and set priorities. Often supervisors are unaware of how much you have to do.

Deadlines: Once again, planning and scheduling will help you track your work flow. When you have a long-range overview written down in a planner or calendar, you can schedule your work at a comfortable pace and thus avoid surprise deadlines. When you have last minute requests with deadlines from your boss, let her know what is already on your agenda and ask her to help you rearrange your schedule. Let your boss have ultimate responsibility for setting priorities and seeing that deadlines are met.

Interpersonal Conflicts: Conflicts arise out of differences in opinions, needs, values and expectations. Stress results because each person involved in the conflict wants things her way, and someone wants to keep her from getting what she wants. We usually think that if one person wins an argument, the other loses. This does not have to be the case. You can reduce the stress of conflict by looking for areas of agreement first. Focus on the task to be accomplished rather than the egos involved. Remember you want to solve a problem. It's not necessary to prove someone else wrong to do this.

Too Much Responsibility Without Authority: It is a good idea to ask for enough authority to carry out your responsibilities in a professional way. When you cannot get that authority, document what you have accomplished and send that memo to your boss. Your memo should include what you need to complete the project. This way you have covered yourself and have let your boss know that you require authority to match your responsibilities.

Speaking Before a Group or Being in the Spotlight: Part of this stressor is fear of making a public mistake and looking foolish. Complete knowledge of your subject matter will give you some confidence. To hone your presentation skills, enroll in a good course on public speaking. That will give you more confidence. Confidence is an antidote to stress. Practice speaking before non-threatening groups to reduce your stress. However, you don't want to get rid of your "butterflies" — you want them to fly in formation.

Wage Inequities, Discrimination and Sexual Harassment in the Workplace: Know your rights under the law. Some of the most stressful discrimination exists in subtle ways and can't be quantified. But often women don't assert themselves in expecting equity and equality. Harriet was hired for the same job as Mark. Two weeks later she discovered that she was being paid considerably less than Mark. When she confronted her employer, he said, "You accepted the salary I offered you. Mark asked for more." Harriet was glad just to get the job and had not been assertive in negotiating for her worth. This is a common trait among working women. Know your worth and your rights. Ask for the treatment — and the money — you deserve.

First Aid for Stressful Times

Stress is a condition of modern life. Even if you live a healthy lifestyle and can deal with most stressful job situations, you will still have periods of frustration and stress. When you need a quick pick-me-up, try these ideas:

- Nicole Schapiro, mentioned previously, has several useful techniques to use when over-stressed. "I surround myself with people who nourish me. I know people to play with, people who stimulate me intellectually and people with whom I can feel comfortable just being quiet.'' Nicole, also an expert on professional image, said, ''Colors affect our moods. When I am under a great deal of pressure, I wear a color that reflects my essence and gives me energy.''

- Make a list of the good things in your life.
- Read something inspirational.
- Go to a chapel or somewhere to sit and pray or meditate.
- Buy yourself a gift or reward. (Stay away from a box of candy.)
- Pamper yourself at a beauty salon. Have a facial, manicure, etc.
- Have a massage.
- Take a hot bubble bath.
- Go to a movie or concert.
- Read fiction or something that has nothing to do with your work.
- Change tasks. If you are mentally tired, do something physical. This is especially important for women who work on computer terminals.
- Watch a baby play.
- Pet a dog or cat.
- Put flowers on your desk, in your bedroom, in your bathroom. Plants are wonderful, but fresh flowers are special.
- Have a non-business lunch with a friend.
- Have refreshments in an outdoor cafe.
- Phone someone who gives you a lift.
- Sit by a fire with a cup of tea.
- Go to the park, watch the ducks in the pond.
- Buy and send a greeting card to someone special.
- Use fine china or crystal for refreshment breaks.
- Repeat to yourself — ''I certainly am a happy person.''

Dr. Hans Selye says that the person who lives in such a way as to earn her neighbor's love is the person who has little negative stress in her life. I like that statement. It's very hard to live that way when there are so many daily pressures on us. However, I have found that an attitude of gratefulness and goodwill toward others eliminates hostility, resentment, jealousy, anger, depression and many of the other negative feelings that influence the behavior of a person under stress. Peace of mind comes from being at peace with others and the environment. It comes from keeping your "I love you's" up-to-date.

Bibliography

Bailey, Covert, *Fit or Fat.* Boston: Houghton Mifflin Company, 1978.

Braiker, Harriet B., "A New Way to Manage Stress That Really Works for Women," *Working Woman,* August 1984.

Cooper, C.L. and Davidson, Marilyn, "The High Cost of Stress on Women Managers," *Organizational Dynamics,* Spring 1982.

Forbes, Rosalind, *Corporate Stress: How to Manage Stress on the Job and Make It Work for You.* Garden City, N.Y.: Doubleday & Co., 1979.

Galton, Lawrence, *Coping With Executive Stress.* New York: McGraw-Hill Book Company, 1983.

Josepfowitz, Natasha, *Is This Where I Was Going?* New York: Warner Books, 1983.

Knight, R. Chris, "Can Stress Make You Sick?" *Working Woman,* April 1984.

Lazarus, Richard S., "Little Hassles Can Be Hazardous to Health," *Psychology Today,* July 1981.

Pelletier, Kenneth R., *Mind As Healer, Mind As Slayer: A Wholistic Approach to Preventing Stress Disorders.* New York: Dell Publishing Company, 1977.

Pinkstaff, Marelen Arthur and Wilkinson, Anna Bell, *Women at Work: Overcoming the Obstacles.* Reading, Mass.: Addison-Wesley Publishing Company, 1979.

Rubin, David, *Everything You Always Wanted to Know About Nutrition.* New York: Avon Books, 1979.

Ryan, Regina Sara and Travis, John W., *Wellness Workbook.* Berkeley: Ten Speed Press, 1981.

Selye, Hans, *The Stress of Life.* New York: McGraw-Hill Book Company, 1978.

Stanford Heart Disease Prevention Program, *Food for Health.* Stanford, Calif.: Stanford University, 1982.

Witkin-Lanoil, Georgia, *The Female Stress Syndrome.* New York: Newmarket Press, 1984.

Step #12
Nurture the Roots of Success

by J.J. Cochran

W e plant the seeds for our own success. But planting is not enough. The seeds must be cared for and cultivated. The tallest, mightiest trees have the deepest roots. Here are the tools you'll need to cultivate your success.

What Do You Really Want?

A righteous and pious woman had fallen into hard times. She said, "God, I need to win the lottery." The next day the lottery was drawn and she did not win. That night she said, "God, I haven't got a job and I need to win the lottery." The next day she found out that she did not win. The third night she said, "Look, God, give me a break, I need to win the lottery!" And God said, "Give Me a break, at least buy a ticket!" Deciding what you want is one way to "buy a ticket."

My general definition of success is going for and getting what one wants, and feeling satisfied with it. We make a commitment to the entire process of going after it. We take risks and act! In the process our idea of what we want may change. That's okay because we receive new information. The process is just as important as the final goal because success is not something we pursue — it's something we attract. And we attract it by our daily lives, by the tools we use rather than just the moment of when we achieve "it." While we may think "it" is what we are aiming for, actually the process says more about who we are and what we're made of. We need persistence to hang in there, to accept "failure" as part of the learning and moving forward. When we do get what we want, we need to delight in it, to accept it, to cherish it, to experience it fully. Then ... move on to the next success.

Attitude Is 80 Percent, Aptitude Is 20 Percent

"There is nothing so good or bad, but thinking makes it so."
                                                                    Shakespeare

Two construction workers are having lunch. The first one opens his lunch box and says, "Oh, no, peanut butter sandwiches again!" The other guy says, "Well, why don't you just tell your wife not to make them?" The first guy replies, "I don't have a wife; I make them for myself."

What are the peanut butter sandwiches you keep feeding yourself even when you no longer want them?

Success begins in our minds. Our lives are affected by the way we *think* things are, not by the way they are. We see what we want to see.

What is your attitude? What conversations do you hold with yourself? Is the little voice inside your head primarily positive or negative? Do you believe in suicide? Most people would answer no; yet constantly berating ourselves every day is a form of suicide. But since it's such a slow death — a slow erasing of our self-esteem and confidence — we fail to perceive it as suicide. Yet, if we dissolve our foundation and our belief in ourselves, we cannot live life to the fullest. Mental suicide is hell.

Your attitude is your choice. Make it an attitude of enthusiasm, thankfulness and "I can!"

Enthusiasm is to a person what electricity is to light or fuel to a car. It "charges" us and makes us go on. The attitude of gratitude is amazing because when we give thanks, we have more room to receive. Try it, it really works. And try filling your mind up with "I can." You'll start to open channels of creativity that would be closed to you if your thoughts centered on "I can't."

The oldest motivational statement in the world is: Whatever the mind can conceive and believe, it can achieve. It's true. Think about any of the accomplishments in your life. First, you thought about the possibility, then you moved beyond the disbelief and started to consider that it was possible. Finally, you figured out ways to accomplish it, even when it seemed totally beyond your reach at the start.

Look at the following words and make a statement with them: it go for. What do you see? For go it or go for it? Totally different attitudes. The choice is yours.

Who's Responsible for Your Life?

"The bottom line is that I am responsible for my own well-being, my own happiness. The choices and decisions I make regarding my life directly influence the quality of my days."

Kathleen Andrus

What was your favorite fairy tale when you were little? Mine was Cinderella. Ah, to be carried off to happy-ever-after-land and be totally cared for. Although we might try to give away the responsibility, the bottom line is, of course, that we are responsible for our own lives. Others may influence us, may try to force us, may "know" what's best for us, yet the decisions and choices belong to us.

You create the world exactly the way you want it. Now you might be thinking, "She doesn't know what I've experienced in my life, and I certainly didn't ask for it or want it." But I do know about those experiences. I didn't create the three sudden deaths of my father, brother and husband within six months of each other when I was 19. But I did create my reaction to their deaths and determined the effect on me.

What did I decide? To show the world I didn't need anybody and I could be great without any help from anyone. That was true. Except I found out it wasn't any fun. While I used that energy to produce and succeed in a traditional definition of that word, my life wasn't balanced. So I re-decided. Now I choose to let people into my life, to get close, to allow myself to need people. I'm still successful — but it's by my definition of that word, which includes feeling good about all the areas in my life, not just career. And you know what? I'm still J.J. The only thing I've changed is my attitude. I now proudly claim responsibility for each attitude and reaction I choose.

I find that idea exciting. Some people find it scary or put themselves down for not having made better decisions in the past. The truth is, we all do the best we can and make the best decisions we know how at the time. Don't abuse yourself with it — use it to your advantage.

We are not the victims of circumstance, but rather the architects. When we get past the "I can't help it," "that's my nature," "I've always been that way" and "that's just me" to accept our responsibility, we start living a creative, joyful life.

The Balance of Ordinary and Extraordinary

"For everything there is a season, and the season is you."
Carol Ruth Knox

Balance is part of the harmony of the universe. We see this principle in day and night, tides and seasons. The bottom line in creating success in our lives is loving ourselves. Part of that self-love is accepting our ordinary and extraordinary parts and balancing the two. We need both.

Ordinary

"Sometimes I think my greatest problem is lack of confidence. I'm scared, and I think that's healthy."
Jane Fonda

Ordinary is a passive state, a place to relax and refresh. It is the place where we get our belonging needs met. Here we need to reach out to others. It's where we accept our humanness, even with mistakes. It's where we come to rest after we've produced in our extraordinary state. It's a place to heal after we've been hurt.

When you get up in the morning, do you look in the mirror and say, "Hello, Beautiful!" or do you say, "Oh, my gosh, I don't believe it!"? I challenge you to look in the mirror tomorrow, look into your eyes and say, "I love you." We have to be able to love ourselves just the way we are. Everything starts here. We can't give love to others any more than we feel love for ourselves. We can't accept other people any more than we accept ourselves. And I don't think we can be any more powerful than how much we love ourselves.

Self-esteem/self-love is the common denominator of success. We need to love the parts we don't like and accept the fact that we are imperfect. Your goals and limitations are affected by your self-image. If you love yourself unconditionally, you'll have the security we all look for, but which can only be found inside ourselves.

When we love ourselves, we give ourselves power. All else starts from this feeling. Then we can move to our extraordinary part.

Extraordinary

"If I had to describe something as divine it would be what happens between people when they really get it together. There is a kind of spark that makes it all worthwhile. When you feel that spark, you get a good feeling deep in your gut."

June L. Tapp

Our extraordinariness is the combination of skills, gifts, talents and qualities that we possess. It's what makes us unique. It's what we have to give to the world. It's the essence of us. Extraordinary is where we believe in ourselves and our possibilities. It's where we nurture, inspire and celebrate ourselves. Extraordinary is a combination of dreams, service, enthusiasm and risk.

Many people are negative about owning their extraordinariness. They have been taught to think that it's bad/conceited/negative to be in touch with what they do so well. I believe the opposite. When we are in touch with the special gift we have to share, then we are in service to the world. We no longer are self-conscious and inwardly focused. When we share our gift we contribute to life.

In 1966 Jim Kaat was a Minnesota Twins pitcher. The Twins had a new coach that year. The coach asked Kaat, "What do you pitch?" Kaat replied, "A fastball, curve, slider and knuckleball." The coach asked, "What is your best pitch?" Kaat said, "My fastball." Then the coach asked him, "What are you going to practice?" Kaat's response was, "My curve, slider and knuckleball." To which the coach replied, "No, you're not. What you're going to practice 90 percent of the time is your fastball." Kaat did. He won 26 games that year! (If you're not a baseball buff, 20 games is what pitchers strive for; 26 is unheard of.) He won Most Valuable Pitcher in the American League that year.

What's your fastball? Wouldn't you be helping your team/company/family more by using it?

Take a realistic appraisal of yourself. Accept your limitations and honor your strengths. Accept your wholeness.

Outrageous Dreams

"There were many ways of breaking a heart, stories were full of hearts broken by love, but what really broke a heart was taking away its dream — whatever that dream might be."

Pearl S. Buck

Fleas, if you put them in a jar, will jump out. If you put on a lid, they will jump up and hit their heads. After several times they will jump up just beneath where the lid is. Then if you take the lid off, they will jump up just beneath where the lid *was* — they won't jump out of the jar!

Without outrageous dreams we stay in that jar.

So write a list of ten or more outrageous dreams. Stretch yourself, let your imagination go wild. Then continue to look at the list. In time, those outrageous dreams won't look so outrageous and you'll start to think of ways to make them become reality.

Outrageous dreams take us outside our normal comfort zone. Without them, we become like fleas.

Life Purpose

"I believe that true identity is found in creative activity springing from within. It is found, paradoxically, when one loses oneself. Woman can best find herself by losing herself in some kind of creative activity of her own."

Anne Morrow Lindbergh

We need a life purpose because there are so many options in the world. Without focusing we become scattered. We don't progress very far because we keep changing direction.

A life purpose helps us focus on the opportunities available to us. Opportunities are always there, it's just that we're more open to seeing and taking advantage of them when we're focused.

A life purpose provides the context and inspiration for our lives. It gives a reason for our existence. It adds meaning to our lives. We all have periods that are rough and we wonder if we will ever get through them. Having a life purpose helps us to move through these hard times. It fills us with enthusiasm. A life purpose helps us realize that our being here means something. It's a way to see beyond the obvious of the "now" to the entire context of our lives. Our life purpose reminds us that we have a contribution to make. Purpose is power.

Having dreams and a purpose enables us to overcome resistance. Have you ever achieved a dream/purpose with no problems, hassles, setbacks or rough edges? I haven't, though some are smoother than others. From my vantage point, these difficulties sometimes look like brick walls — impossible to break through. Actually, they provide an opportunity for us to grow by resolving our deepest fears. Typically, I find that my brick walls are just paper with bricks drawn on. And on the other side of every paper brick wall is more light, joy, intimacy and trust. Once we're willing to walk through fear, we transform it into power. We move forward. However, without dreams and a life purpose, we wouldn't be willing to take those risks. The dreams and purpose give us a place to focus so we can move through the learning and on to the next step in the process.

A personal example relates to starting my own business. I did not start in an ideal situation when everything was "right." (Who does? But often we keep waiting until the "right" time. We could wait forever with that attitude.) Since I was a speaker and was paid per engagement, some months money rolled in, some months there was no money at all! There were times when I didn't eat or I couldn't pay bills. Each time I asked myself, "Am I in the right field?" (and my speaking is a part of my life purpose) or "Am I doing the right thing or is this a hint to give up?" Each time I replied that it was "right." My life purpose and tenacity helped me keep going. We all have fears and roadblocks. Successful people are the ones who keep going. Life purpose helps in that forward direction.

From life purpose we move to goals. Goals provide the content of our lives and the motivation. We break down goals into activities. However, most of us do many activities that are scattered. If we hit a goal, we're lucky. And whoever heard of a life goal? It's like the talk Alice in Wonderland had with the Cheshire cat. She asked him, "Which way should I go?" He answered, "Well, where are you going?" Alice said, "I don't know." The Cheshire cat grinned and replied, "Well, it doesn't much matter then, does it?"

Terry Fox provides a good example. He was a young Canadian who lost a leg to cancer. When that happened, he decided to make his life's purpose to help eradicate cancer. His goal was to run across Canada at the rate of one marathon a day to collect one million dollars for cancer research. He had major obstacles to overcome: people's disbelief, cold weather, lack of media attention, and many others. He ran three-fifths of the way across Canada before becoming ill. Cancer had spread throughout his body and he died. He also had collected 24 million dollars for cancer research!

There's a film about him, *The Power of Purpose,* produced by David McNally. This film was not made to make Terry a hero. It was made to get people in touch with how the power of purpose can help us accomplish more in our lives.

If you don't have a life purpose, now is the time to figure it out. Imagine yourself shortly before you die being interviewed about your life. You're telling the interviewer all the important times in your life. Since you're not there yet, obviously, you can make up anything. What would you like to be remembered for? What was important? It can be big or small, personal or professional, as long as it is what *you* want. Doing this exercise gives you an idea of what you want in your life. You can use this to help you make daily decisions by asking yourself, "Does this fit in with my life purpose?"

Ideal Day

"The wisdom of all ages and cultures emphasizes the tremendous power our insights have over our character and circumstances."
Diane Cordes

Another way to help us learn what we think is important in our lives is to imagine an ideal work day or ideal non-work day, one year, five years, not more than ten years into the future. Close your eyes and let yourself imagine the day in detail. Use all of your senses. Where are you? What are you doing? Who are you with? What kind of lifestyle do you have? How much money do you make? How do you spend it? Etc., etc. After about fifteen minutes open your eyes and write down what you imagined.

Those specifics give you an idea of the content of your life. If you look deeper you will find the context for your life — the values, hopes and dreams. This gives you a good idea of where you want to go. Then look at your life and see where you are. Are the things you're doing in your life now leading you toward your ideal day or away from it? If it is away, you need to re-evaluate what you are doing. When you want to change your life, there is only you and there is only now. What will you do? The future does not get better by hope, but by plan.

Courage

"Do the thing you fear and the death of fear is certain."
Ralph Waldo Emerson

When we decide upon our life purpose and our direction, we're bombarded by our fears and reasons why we cannot do this. What is your "but..."? We all have them. The point here is not to resist, ignore, avoid, fight, condemn or retreat from our fears. Move through them. How? With courage.

When you order, command or demand that some fear in you disappear, you set in motion a counterforce that comes in the form of rebellion, sabotage or fear of failing. When we resist, it persists. Our resistance keeps us from recognizing our opportunities by increasing tensions, keeping us from growing and giving fear power over us.

We change fears with courage: the courage to look, to acknowledge, to experience. Then we courageously decide what to do and start acting on it. With courage we can accept even those parts of us we don't want to. With gentleness we can be kind and patient with ourselves in this process. It takes time. And the courage to hang in there.

Here is a story of courage. King Christian was the King of Denmark during World War II. The Nazis told the king that the Jews must wear armbands, and thus be singled out for persecution. King Christian could have resisted and said, "No," which would have caused problems for everyone. Or he could have ignored the obvious and submitted to his fear by having the Jews wear armbands. Instead, he chose to surrender to his fear. He said, "Since it's so good, we will *all* wear armbands." Surrender with courage to your fears and you will move through them.

The Power of Believing

"As a person thinketh in her heart, so she is."

Anonymous

You become what you think. It's your choice what and how you believe. You create into existence what you believe. We have the tools and capability to create extraordinary lives despite the fact that most of us choose mediocre ones. Our belief and our faith determine who we are and who we become more than anything else.

Napoleon Hill, author of *Think and Grow Rich* and *Laws of Success*, says, "You have absolute control over but one thing — your thoughts. This divine prerogative is the sole means by which you may control your destiny. If you fail to control your mind, you will control nothing else. Your mind is your spiritual estate.''

What you hold in your mind today will shape your experiences of tomorrow. What do you have faith in? You? Something greater? What you have faith in determines your life. If you believe in a universal source you can tap into, then that is what you will get. If you have faith in only yourself, then those are the benefits you will reap. Either way you will produce. But one way is easier and limitless.

The tools of belief are visualization and affirmation. We use them every day. However, most of us use them negatively. Just as the oak is within the acorn, the potential for our lives lies within.

Visualization is picturing in your mind an outcome. What we visualize determines what comes to fruition because our minds do not know the difference between an actual and an imagined event. Superior athletes use visualization to help them achieve. They imagine themselves winning on the court or field or wherever they perform. Those thoughts fill the mind and subconscious and get acted upon.

A study was done where students were divided into three groups. The control group did nothing for four weeks. A second group practiced shooting baskets. The third group imagined shooting baskets. In retesting, the control group showed no change. The group that practiced shooting baskets was 23 percent better. And the group that imagined shooting baskets was 23 percent better! Your mind does not know the difference between an imagined event and an actual event.

What are you putting into your mind? When you have a new or scary task, do you imagine it exactly how you want it to turn out? Or do you imagine all the worst possible consequences? And then what happens? If you had a rough day or an argument or lost a sale, do you keep repeating in your mind how bad it was and how wrong you were? Or do you imagine how you would have liked it to have been? Your mind will follow whatever you put into it.

What words do you say to yourself? We all have a little voice inside that critiques everything we do and is usually a harsh judge. Do you listen to this voice or have you learned how to turn it off, or at least down?

I remember when I used to believe I was a trainer but would never be a speaker. They are quite different styles. I woke up on my thirtieth birthday and my first thought was, "I am a speaker." I wondered where that came from and then realized, "Of course, I can't be a speaker without first thinking it." I started saying the affirmation (a positive statement that one repeats to oneself often): "I am a speaker. I am a speaker. I am a speaker..." At first, that little voice that tries to sabotage me kept saying, "You are a liar. You are a liar. You are a liar..." But the positive affirmation outlasted the little voice and was a first step in my becoming a speaker.

What is your belief about yourself? If you are not sure, just take a look at your life. What you have today is the direct result of what you created in your mind yesterday.

Take the Initiative to Act

"Even if you're on the right track, you'll get run over if you just sit there."
                                                                    Will Rogers

We've talked about figuring out what we want; creating an attitude that supports that; taking responsibility for our lives; realizing how human and how extraordinary we are; defining our life purpose; handling our fears with courage, and using the universal techniques of visualization and affirmation to get a clear picture of what we want. However, all of that does us little good unless we are willing to act.

A 95-year-old man and a 93-year-old woman walked into the divorce lawyer's office. They told her, "We want a divorce." She inquired, "How long have you been married?" They replied brusquely, "Fifty-two years," in voices that implied it had been a *long* fifty-two years. The lawyer asked, "Why do you want a divorce now?" They replied that they had always wanted a divorce. "Well, why did you wait until now?" she asked with some amazement. "We were waiting for the children to die."

What are you waiting for? What is your "if only..."? What will it take for you to get off your "but" and move into action?

An old Chinese proverb says, "A journey of 10,000 miles begins with a single step." Positive thoughts need to be followed with positive action. Perhaps the statement, "You are what you think," should be amended to, "You are what you think — and do." How often have we waited to start something until the time was "right" or until we could do it perfectly? Moving and failing is a lesson that gives you more information to work with than not ever moving in the first place. Go for it — NOW!

Boldness

"Life is either a daring adventure or nothing."

Helen Keller

We remember Babe Ruth as the home run king. What we often forget is that he was also the strikeout king. He was bold at the plate. He took risks. And it paid off for him. It can pay off for you, too. If you're not willing to fail, then you're not willing to succeed.

Bruce Larson interviewed leading thinkers from several disciplines on the subject of human wholeness and wellness. He asked their opinion of what was a common, necessary ingredient for wellness. The bottom line from these folks was the ability to take a healthy risk.

Risk opens us up, saves us from boredom and stagnation, keeps us reaching higher. It moves us on. It is the basis of mental health and growth. The turtle moves forward only when it sticks out its neck.

Of course, sometimes it's smart not to risk. I remember watching platform diving on TV. The participants were probably 100 feet in the air, diving into a pool made especially for those heights. Last year's champion was taking his final dive and everyone expected him to win. He climbed up, prepared to dive — and then didn't. He climbed down. He later told reporters that he just could not do it anymore; he had reached his limit. Realize where your limits are and respect them. I admired him for having the boldness to say, "No, I choose not to do this." He respected his own inner knowing. Trust yours as well.

When the time is ripe for you to move forward, take it — even if a part of you is scared. Focus on the reward rather than on the avoidance. Think of the times you have moved through your fears with boldness and how that has enhanced your life. Make risk your friend.

Commitment

"There are no great people, there is only great commitment."

Anonymous

A chicken and a pig were out taking a morning stroll. They came across a cafe and decided to stop for breakfast. The special was ham and eggs. The chicken said, "We'll take two." The pig turned white. The chicken asked, "What's the matter?" The pig said, "For you, it's a contribution; for me, it's a total commitment!"

What are you totally committed to? Often we have to be willing to let go of other things. Once we are committed, amazing things happen. We see opportunities we never noticed before. Goethe's poem aptly describes this phenomenon:

Until one is committed
there is always hesitancy, the chance to draw back,
always ineffectiveness.

Concerning all acts of initiative (and creation)
there is one elementary truth
the ignorance of which kills countless ideas
and splendid plans.

That the moment one definitely commits oneself
then Providence moves too.

All sorts of things occur to help one
that would never otherwise have occurred.

A whole stream of events issues from the decision
raising in one's favour all manner
of unforeseen incidents and meetings
and material assistance
which no man [woman] could have dreamt
would have come his [her] way.

Whatever you can do or dream you can, begin it.
Boldness has genius, power and magic in it.

Begin it now.

Besides helping us see opportunities we would otherwise have missed, having a commitment also helps us stick out the rough times by helping us focus on the results we want rather than the present uncomfortableness.

Having commitment works like the scene from the movie *The Natural*. It's the bottom of the ninth and the bases are loaded. It's the championship game. The "Natural" has two strikes against him and has just broken his favorite, lifetime bat. He is also in great physical pain. But he perseveres, and in great Hollywood style, hits a grand slam. They may look like fairy tales, but we can accomplish great things in our lives when we are committed.

Tenacity

"Everyone has talent. What is rare is the courage to follow the talent to the dark place where it leads."
Erica Jong

Commitment helps us hang in there, which brings us to the next root of success: tenacity. Tenacity is the willingness to keep going even when the going gets rough. Tenacity goes beyond talent and skill or intelligence. It is something that all of us can tap into and it can create the difference between success and failure.

When Napoleon Hill talked with over 500 successful people, he found that each had become successful after a major defeat. It wasn't that they had more capacity for success. They had the tenacity to stick out the rough times. It seems to be the universe's way of weeding people out. Defeat is the test for us to decide what we really want. It helps us become clear about what we want and whether it's worth the time and effort. If we pass the test, we succeed.

The lack of tenacity reminds me of a scene in the movie *Fame*. One young woman was in dance class trying very hard. At one point the teacher comes by and says, "I don't see any sweat." Finally the teacher tells her she can no longer be a dance major. The scene switches to the subway station where it looks like the student is going to commit suicide by throwing herself in front of an oncoming train. At the very last instant she throws her dance gear in front of the train and says, "I'll become a theater major." But she probably won't succeed at that either because she is not willing to work hard for anything.

Often we get impatient and want it all right now. However, there are reasons for our growth. Often we find out later why the time we had to wait was good for us. Patience is a trait that Edison had. Do you know how many times he tried combinations for the filament for the light bulb before he got the right one? Take a guess. Ten? One hundred? Five thousand? No, 10,000 times! He said he hadn't failed 9999 times, he had just learned how *not* to do it.

Are you a salesperson? Have you ever had one of those rainy days and you figure that no one will buy so you are not even going out? Have you ever noticed that lone salesperson out on that day makes all the sales and is a top producer? We have to be willing to put up with rainy days or slow times or not-so-perfect circumstances in order to get what we want. Tenacity is the quality that all successful people possess. Its power is told in the following statement. "If you really want it, nothing can keep you from it; if you don't, anything will." (Author unknown.)

Seeing Problems as Opportunities and Challenges

"Courage is the price life exacts for granting peace."
Amelia Earhart

Think of a waterfall. Now take a few moments and write down your experience of a waterfall. Do you like it? Most of us do. What adjectives did you use? Our "negative" life experiences are like a waterfall. There is the fall over the edge — our experience. Then there is the calm. Then it harnesses energy and moves on to create great things. We can do that with life's experiences, too. We have our fall and sometimes we think it's over and we wonder if we will survive. However, if we experience the fall, then we move into the calm and start to integrate what we learned. We can then take what we've learned and move on to our greater good.

Think about the uncomfortable events in your life. You may not have liked them and you probably would not ask for them again, yet haven't you noticed that once you are all the way through them your life is better than it was before? That is how it is with our "negative" experiences.

Use that information for the next problem which comes into your life. Immediately relabel the problem an opportunity or a challenge. We learn in life from our experiences and often we learn more from negative ones than positive ones. Growth is a process. So even though negative events may look like temporary setbacks, they end up moving us on, opening us up, teaching us new skills and enhancing our qualities. They empower us.

When negative experiences happen, remember and believe that in each situation there is the seed of equal or greater good. Spring always follows winter. Keep looking for the spring in the situation. It is not what happens to us in life that counts, but what we do with what happens.

A Norwegian fisherman was out in the ocean with his two sons catching fish. A storm came up and they became lost. It looked like this was the end for them. Then they saw a light in the distance. They did not know what it was or where it was, but they headed toward it, figuring the light meant safety. Indeed, they did get to shore. The fisherman was met by his wife who was in tears because their house had just burned down and with it everything they owned. When she told her husband, he did not respond. She said, "Didn't you hear me? Everything we have is lost!" And he replied softly, "We were lost at sea and thought we wouldn't survive. We saw a light in the distance and followed it. We arrived on shore safely. Our burning house was the light that brought us home."

James Allen in *As a Man Thinketh* finishes this thought by saying: "To put away aimlessness and weakness, and to begin to think with purpose, is to enter the ranks of those strong ones who only recognize failure as one of the pathways to attainment; who make all conditions serve them, and who think strongly, attempt fearlessly, and accomplish masterfully."

Point of View or Reframing

"Follow your dream ... Take one step at a time and don't settle for less, just continue to climb ... if you stumble, don't stop and lose sight of your goal, press on to the top. For only on top can we see the whole view."

Amanda Bradley

A woman wanted to prove the evils of alcohol. She went to a meeting and took with her a vat of water, a vat of alcohol and a worm. She put the worm in the water and the worm swam around. Then she took out the worm and dropped it into the alcohol. The worm disintegrated. She stepped back, folded her arms and asked rather haughtily, "What does that prove?" A woman in the back raised her hand and said, "It proves that if you drink you don't get worms." Well, that is one way to look at it. And it illustrates the point about reframing, one of the most powerful tools we have.

Reframing is a root of success over which we have total control. It is completely internal and we can create it in our minds however we want. This is how it works. First, there is an event. Then we give a context to the event. The context and the event equal our experience of the event. If we don't like our experience of the event and we can't change the event, the only thing we have total control over is the context.

An example of this would be blind people feeling an elephant and describing it to each other. One says, "There's a long thing here that sways back and forth and is wet on the end." Another says, "Are you kidding? There's just a big stalk here." Another replies, "There's a big wall here, it's curved and there's no end to it." And still another comments, "All I feel is a very thick strand like a piece of rope that sways back and forth." And *they're all right!* It is their point of view. If they stepped two feet to the right or five feet to the left they would have a different point of view.

You can do the same thing in your life. Any event can have an infinite number of responses. Choose the one you want. Every time I have an uncomfortable event or one that I do not like, I immediately ask myself, "What can I learn from this? How can I hold this so it ends up being positive?" That doesn't mean that

I ignore my discomfort or pretend I am not angry or hurt. What it does mean is that I accept that it has happened and I put it in a context or overall view that makes it easier to comprehend. With that frame of reference, I allow myself to do what I need to do. That might be crying or confronting someone else or asking for help or moving ahead. Whatever. The following story illustrates the point of view that whatever happens is for our highest good.

In Louisiana a mule fell into a 40 foot well. The farmer did not know how to get the mule out. He decided to put the animal out of its misery, figuring it had been hurt in the fall. The only thing he could think to do was to bury the mule in the well. He dumped dirt on the mule. However, with each load, the mule stamped on it and raised himself up until he could walk away. The mule instinctively knew what some of us are beginning to learn. The very thing designed to finish us off can be used, through faith, to bring us out on top.

Acceptance and Forgiveness

"Don't fight the darkness. Let it envelope you, like a womb, and grow you."
J. J. Cochran

One of the ingredients in turning problems into opportunities is point of view. Another is acceptance.

Again, if we resist something, it persists. The easiest way to move through something, even though it is a paradox, is to sit in it, experience it and accept it. Then move through it and forward.

We can use this for ourselves in our growth process. As we grow we are like a snake that sheds its skin, or a butterfly freeing itself from the cocoon. As we transform, we need to release the old parts of us to make room for the new parts. However, we need to be careful about how we do this process.

As we heal, we release old parts of ourselves. This does not mean disowning, repressing or throwing away parts of ourselves. Humility is an acceptance of all parts of us and loving us as we are right now. I believe those parts we don't like are defenses we built for protection. They were created when somewhere along the line we were scolded, rejected, teased or didn't measure up. They have served us well trying to protect us from further pain.

But they have also taken their toll, especially in our adulthood. I believe those parts are parts that must be loved. If we try to disown them they will fight and hang on. But if we accept and love those parts and appreciate their protection, then we will be able to transform that energy into one that is more appropriate for us now. Releasing is a process of acceptance first and then transformation of energy.

Along with acceptance comes forgiveness, of ourselves and others. When we don't forgive, we feel deprived, have less energy, increase our defense systems, create ongoing bitterness, feel left out, want revenge and feel resentful. All of this binds us and focuses us away from our life purpose. The only person you hurt by keeping a grudge is yourself. The other person probably doesn't even know that you have the grudge. You hurt your own system with that bitterness.

Forgiving ourselves is equally important. Inner peace is knowing that the key to life is not to find a meaningful place, but to find meaning in the place where you are. Acceptance and forgiveness help us do that.

Sharing: Supporting Others and Letting Them Support You

"Often when we're being tough and strong, we're scared. It takes a lot of courage to allow ourselves to be vulnerable, to be soft."
Dudley Martineau

A lion was walking through the jungle and asking every animal it came upon, "Who is king of the jungle?" The monkey replied, "You." So did the giraffe and the gazelle. But when the lion asked the elephant, the elephant did not reply, but instead picked up the lion in its trunk and thrashed him around, finally putting him back on the ground. The lion stood up and said, "Well, you don't have to get shook just because you don't know the answer!"

How many times do we get shook because we don't know the answer? Our society, especially for women now with the superwoman syndrome, teaches us that it's good to be totally self-reliant.

But there comes a time when we must let other people in.

We are here and we are human. Part of the human condition is needing each other. Remember ordinary? We all are ordinary and part of that is our need for belonging. I learned how wonderful support can be during a time of personal trial. In past traumatic situations I decided I could do it alone. However, when the most recent one happened I was overwhelmed and knew I needed help. What I found out was surprising to me. I had always learned that to be "good," to be "lovable," I had to achieve great things — by myself. However, I learned that people loved me just as much when I asked for help, and actually felt closer to me because of it. My friends said, "J.J., we always thought you were perfect, and we thought we had to be perfect to be around you. Since we knew we weren't perfect, we withdrew. We don't like seeing you hurt but we do like seeing you human and asking for help." I actually increased the intimacy in my life and felt how wonderful it is to get support.

Of course, we also can give to others in less needy times. That's the idea of networking, mentoring and sponsoring. It is sharing what we have with people — ideas, time, a place to bounce off ideas, experience, "know-how." Each person need not reinvent the wheel. Instead, we can share our wheels to make a wagon and the next person can make a car and so on...

As we give, we receive. It doesn't mean that we receive the same from the person to whom we gave. In the long run, though, we get back from the world more than we give. Giving at first may be difficult. Take for example when I started my own consulting business. One of my primary areas of expertise is knowing how to open conventions, energize meetings and get audience participation. Sometimes people did not want to hire me but they would call for exercises and information on how to move their groups. At first I did not want to share that information because I thought if I gave it out, what would be the point of their ever hiring me? However, I realized that I had to live out the values I discuss in my workshops, including the win-win philosophy and sharing with others. So I shared. It was not easy at first. Then it became easier. Amazingly, but not surprisingly, the more I am willing to share information, the more people give to me. I have gained so much from people mentoring me in the last few years. I do not give in order to get, yet that is the way it turns out. I receive more than I give.

We move farther with teamwork. It is surprising that in most corporations, departments see other departments as the "enemy" and something to fight against rather than "we are all in this together." Teamwork may not be as glamorous as having one charismatic leader, but in the long run it produces more. Geese are a good example of this. When they fly, they fly in formation, and the head goose gets the head winds, obviously the roughest spot. They change head geese every couple of miles. By doing so they fly 72 percent farther. Seventy-two percent! With teamwork we are more likely to accomplish our life purpose.

Ask yourself when was the last time you asked for help. Are you willing to acknowledge your strengths and realize that you have areas to grow? Can you let other people fill in those spots with their strengths? Are you willing to give to others? Are you willing to receive?

Ty Boyd tells a story which illustrates support and sharing. Someone made a bet that two young girls couldn't walk a mile on railroad ties without falling off. They took the bet. One got on one railroad tie, the other little girl got on the other tie, and then they reached out their hands. They held hands the entire way and made it because they balanced each other.

The Garden

"Transformation is not a matter of mind; it is a matter of contacting one's inner holiness and letting that shape the personality."
Carol Ruth Knox

By using all these tools, and being patient and kind to ourselves, we, like a tree, create roots in our lives. These roots take hold and give us a firm, unshakable foundation. It is our foundations — our roots — that enable us to succeed.

Plant the seeds you want to create the life you want. I see you as a great, productive, flowering tree.

HOW YOU CAN GET AHEAD WITH CAREERTRACK

Request your FREE CareerTrack catalog of seminars and tapes...

From communication skills, to self-management, to career success strategies, CareerTrack brings you a message of excellence, productivity, imagination and pride.

Founded in 1982 by Jimmy Calano and Jeff Salzman, CareerTrack is the largest business seminar company in North America. Hundreds of thousands of success-oriented professionals look to CareerTrack for the get-ahead information they need. CareerTrack presents over 2000 seminars a year in more than 350 cities throughout the United States, Canada and Australia. It also offers private programs presented to your people at your convenience. Its sister company, CareerTrack Publications, publishes audio and video tapes on a wide range of self-help and professional-development topics.

For your free catalog of CareerTrack's seminars and tapes, just return the coupon below.

☐ **YES! I want to receive a FREE CareerTrack catalog.**

NAME _____

ADDRESS _____

CITY _____ STATE _____ ZIP _____

Mail to **CareerTrack, Inc.** • **1800 38th Street** • **Boulder, CO 80301.** Or call **(303) 447-2300.**

– CLIP OR PHOTOCOPY –

Three Essential Books for the Professional Woman on the Way Up

___ **REACH YOUR CAREER DREAMS!** $15.95
The Essential Handbook for Professional Women   ($22.50, Canada)
by CareerTrack's Highest-Rated Seminar Trainers
Have your own team of expert advisors for making your career dreams come true. From setting realistic goals, to boosting your self-image, to communicating with authority, to networking for advancement — *Reach Your Career Dreams!* — is a powerful, fun-to-read, easy-to-put-into-action handbook that can literally change your life. *(220 pages, hardcover)*

___ **ADVANCED CAREER STRATEGIES FOR WOMEN** $15.95
How to Make It to the Top Faster   ($22.50, Canada)
by Marilyn Machlowitz, Ph.D.
This is the career book for women already climbing the success ladder. It's *not* about how to break into the corporate world — but how to make it to the top. In 40 crisp chapters, Machlowitz (the nationally-known career columnist), presents strategies that are working for today's most successful professional women. Topics range from gaining visibility inside and outside your company, to career-pathing, to understanding corporate politics — and much more. *(212 pages, hardcover)*

___ **PERSONAL POWER** $15.95
The Guide to Power for Today's Working Woman   ($22.50, Canada)
by Arleen LaBella and Dolores Leach
Are you uncomfortable having to take charge of certain situations? Do people resist or even ignore you when you try to exercise power? With this best-selling book, learn the *attitudes of power:* how to look, think and act like a high-achiever. You'll also gain the *tools of power:* risk-taking, decision-making, power communication, competition and collaboration. *(184 pages, hardcover)*

_____ **IT'S EASY TO ORDER** _____

Please send me the book(s) I've checked.
My method of payment is: Total amount of order $ _____
☐ Check (payable to CareerTrack Publications, Inc.)   Check # _____
☐ Please charge to the following credit card:
   ☐ VISA   ☐ MASTERCARD   ☐ AMEX   Exp. Date

Credit Card Number   Month   Year

Cardholder's signature
Please ship to:

NAME _____

ADDRESS _____
          (PLEASE, NO P.O. BOXES.)
CITY _____ STATE _____ ZIP _____

DAY PHONE (_____) _____ EXT. _____

Please allow 3-4 weeks for delivery. Mail payment with order form to:
CareerTrack Publications • 1800 38th Street • Boulder, CO 80301.
Or call (303) 447-2300.

YOUR GUARANTEE: If the products you order are not to your liking, please return them within 15 days. Tell us whether you want a replacement or a full refund and we will get it to you promptly.

— CLIP OR PHOTOCOPY —